Recipes from my
Vietnamese
Kitchen

Recipes from my
Vietnamese Kitchen

AUTHENTIC
FOOD TO
AWAKEN THE
SENSES & FEED
THE SOUL

Uyen Luu

PHOTOGRAPHY BY CLARE WINFIELD

RYLAND PETERS & SMALL
LONDON • NEW YORK

Uyên Lưu hosts Vietnamese supper clubs in her East London studio where she cooks dishes she learned from her mother. She passes on this knowledge of home cooking through her Vietnamese cooking classes. Uyên is a food writer, contributing to various UK publications, including *The Observer Food Monthly*. She lives and works in London as a food photographer.

Visit www.uyenluu.com for information on supper clubs, cooking classes and photography. Follow her @loveleluu on Instagram.

Clare Winfield is a photographer specializing in food. Her work has appeared in magazines, books and on packaging. For Ryland Peters & Small, she has also photographed *Recipes from My Indian Kitchen*, *Two's Company* and *Home Bird*.

SENIOR DESIGNER Megan Smith
COMMISSIONING EDITOR Céline Hughes
PRODUCTION MANAGER Gordana Simakovic
CREATIVE DIRECTOR Leslie Harrington
EDITORIAL DIRECTOR Julia Charles
PUBLISHER Cindy Richards
FOOD STYLIST Uyên Lưu
PROP STYLIST Jo Harris
INDEXER Hilary Bird

First published in 2013 as *My Vietnamese Kitchen*. This edition published in 2024 by Ryland Peters & Small
20–21 Jockey's Fields
London WC1R 4BW
and
341 East 116th Street
New York, NY 10029
www.rylandpeters.com

10 9 8 7 6 5 4 3 2 1

Food photography by Clare Winfield
Travel photography by Uyên Lưu

Text © Uyên Lưu 2013, 2019, 2024
Design and commissioned photographs © Ryland Peters & Small 2013, 2019, 2024

Printed in China

ISBN: 978-1-78879-550-0

NOTES
• All spoon measurements are level unless otherwise specified.
• Ovens should be preheated to the specified temperature. Recipes in this book were tested using a regular oven. If using a fan-assisted oven, follow the manufacturer's instructions for adjusting temperatures.
• All eggs are medium (UK) or large (US), unless otherwise specified. Recipes containing raw or partially cooked egg, or raw fish or shellfish, should not be served to the very young, very old, anyone with a compromised immune system or pregnant women.
• If you are concerned about eating raw beansprouts, cook them before serving.

A CIP record for this book is available from the British Library.

US Library of Congress Cataloging-in-Publication data has been applied for.

FSC
MIX
Paper | Supporting responsible forestry
FSC® C008047
www.fsc.org

Contents

Foreword

I first met Uyen Luu during the filming of my television series, How to Cook Well, when I cooked with her in her small kitchen. We cooked some lovely dishes inspired by her own culture and family, and I remember them with enormous pleasure when flicking through the pages of this, her first book, with Clare Winfield's mouthwatering photographs.

I adore everything about Vietnamese food. Maybe it's the Frenchman in me – and France has had a longer, stronger connection with Vietnam than the colonial one that lasted from 1887 to 1954 – but I'm excited by the fragrance, the beauty, the texture and the multiplicity of flavours of Vietnamese dishes.

Even more than the *bánh mì* stuffed baguette and the sweet milky coffee that are so obviously French-inspired, I relish the aroma of a steaming bowl of *phở*, with its notes of star anise, coriander seeds, hints of cinnamon and cloves, and fresh, fruity notes of herbs and citrus. The warmth of the broth is complemented perfectly by the bite of the noodles.

And how can you not love summer rolls? The pink of the prawns and green herbs showing through the translucent rice-paper wrap promise the lovely contrast of crunchy and smooth textures and fresh, savoury flavours.

Uyen Luu sets this wonderful cuisine in the context of her own family and kitchen. She tells us exactly what ingredients are needed for the most authentic experience of Vietnamese food (and we can be grateful that so many of these ingredients are now available in Britain, thanks to the Vietnamese emigrants who have settled here). But she is not a fusspot: she even gives her own, playful recipe for spaghetti Bolognese – and you have to look carefully at it to spot the splash of fish sauce that gives it a tiny Vietnamese twist. Her fish and chips variation involves raw tuna. Wonderful!

Playfulness is a characteristic of this book. It encourages readers to eat like the Vietnamese do themselves, not worrying too much about the distinctions between meals and snacks.

I assure you, from my own experience, that it really is possible to breakfast on a bowl of spicy noodle soup and feel the better for it all day long. Perhaps it's the notion that food is fun, and eating can be playful, that preserves Vietnam from the Western plague of obesity.

Among her recipes here you'll find many for sustainable species of fish; and you might also notice that her recipes (and this is true for most Vietnamese cooking) are not lavish with energy. This is ethical eating.

Certainly Uyen Luu has learned from her mother to search for a balance of yin and yang in her cooking and diet. This means creating a balance of taste and texture as well as of the traditional heating and cooling properties assigned to foodstuffs. More important than the details of the nutritional theory, though, is the underlying belief that what we eat affects our health – something we in the West have discovered relatively recently, very much to the cost of our physical wellbeing. Moreover, Uyen points out that what we eat (and how and when we eat) also affects our emotional wellbeing, an insight we'd do well to remember.

Raymond Blanc

"Eat playfully"

I was born in Sài Gòn into a family who loves food. In the late 1970s and early 1980s after the Vietnam War, the country fell into extreme poverty and many people had their businesses, livelihoods, land and properties stripped away. There was a trade embargo, and food was scarce or even unavailable.

My grandmother, my father's mother, was a great entrepreneur. In order to support her family in Sài Gòn, she opened up her front room, which led onto the street, to sell *bún bò huế*, the best noodle soup I ever remember eating.

My earliest childhood memory, which I savour, is of the taste and character of that soup. I sat on my little table in the corner and watched my grandmother serve bowl after bowl. She always smiled at the customers. I can recall watching her somewhere among the clouds of lemongrass-scented steam that surrounded her stall: her hair up in a bun, she was a round and handsomely chubby woman who would sniff me whenever I came near. The Vietnamese sniff to kiss.

Since we took refuge in London after the war, I have learnt everything about Vietnamese cooking from my mother, who raised me and my brother on a strict Vietnamese diet so that we would never forget where we came from and so that we would grow up with a sense of belonging. Vietnamese cuisine is one of the most flavoursome in the world, bursting with tangy freshness, sweet tastiness and umami spiciness! When cooking a Vietnamese dish, most of the work is in the preparation rather than on the stove, with many of its basic principles based on satisfying every taste bud.

Preparing and cooking Vietnamese food is about fine-tuning your tasting skills to balance and master sweet, sour, salty, umami, bitter and hot flavours. It is about combining perfect textures, such as silky meat or fish with crunchy vegetables or herbs to satisfy the bite. It is also important to combine and balance ingredients that pair well with each other, and people remain loyal to their tried-and-tested combinations.

It is important to accomplish a perfect harmony of taste, texture and lightness of being. Many people naturally follow the yin and yang ideology in combining ingredients. For example, a soup with hearty ginger to warm up the body is contrasted with refreshing, cool leaves like bok choy to bring a sense of concord. Eating in balance is a major factor in keeping healthy and many believe that food is medicine.

Vietnam has taken much inspiration from its occupiers, especially the French. The streets buzz with a dazzling variety of food and its aromas, from barbecued meat-filled baguettes (*bánh mì*), hot pork pastries, crunchy carrot salads and beef steaks with French fries.

Living in one of the most fertile countries in the world, the Vietnamese make great use of all the vegetation that the land so abundantly offers. Meat and fish are usually luxuries: a family of five will share one fish per family. Therefore, herbs, fruit and vegetables such as morning glory, taro stem/elephant ear, lotus roots, watercress, pineapple, tomatoes and cucumbers fill out a delicious meal, making the diet quite a healthy one.

Vietnamese people love eating so much that they have a term called "*ăn chơi*", which means "to eat playfully", or "to snack". There are many small and light streetfood portions that you can pick up and eat on the go, throughout the day.

The meal doesn't consist of courses; there is no starter/appetizer, main/entrée or dessert. There are snacks, meals in one dish, and family meals with many plates all served at once. Vietnamese food is all about the love of food, flavour and eating. Or in other words, food is love.

Ingredients
Herbs

The Vietnamese use herbs in abundance. Full of perfume, flavour and health benefits, they are used in almost every savoury dish. Coriander/cilantro, Thai sweet basil and mint are the most readily available, so if in doubt, use those. Find out when your nearest Asian store has their fresh vegetable delivery and try to buy your herbs that day.

1. COCKSCOMB MINT (*kinh giới*), also known as Vietnamese lemon balm, resembles minty lemon balm and is used in summer rolls, salads, fish and chicken dishes, and as a garnish in noodle soups. Also great with boiling water as a tea. Alternative herb: lemon balm, available from garden centres.

2. VIETNAMESE CELERY LEAVES (*rau cần*), both the narrow stems and strongly flavoursome leaves of which are used plentifully as a garnish. Stems are usually cooked.

3. PANDAN LEAVES (*lá dứa*) are narrow and long, with a distinct grassy flavour. Used in tea, rice and desserts, and as a green food dye. The leaves can be wrapped around food for grilling or steaming.

4. SAWTOOTH (*ngò gai*) tastes like intense coriander/cilantro and basil in one. Commonly used as a garnish in *phở* or with beef salad.

5. THAI SWEET BASIL (*húng quế*) acts as a garnish in noodle soups such as *phở* and *bún bò Huế*. The leaves taste and smell like aniseed, unlike European basil. Translates from the Vietnamese as "cinnamon basil" and originates from Thailand and Vietnam.

6. HOT MINT (*rau răm*) has a citrus coriander/cilantro aroma reminiscent of, but not related to, mint. Also known as Vietnamese coriander/cilantro, it is commonly eaten raw in salads, as well as in some soups.

7. LEMONGRASS (*xả*) is central to many dishes, from soups to stews and curries. It adds a zesty aroma and a zingy tang to give kick and flavour. It also boasts many health benefits.

8. CURLY MORNING GLORY (*rau muống*) has stems that are sliced into curly threads to be eaten raw in salads and as a garnish in many noodle soups for added crunch and texture.

9. GARLIC CHIVES (*lá hẹ*), also known as Chinese chives, taste very garlicky and are used to season noodle soups, salads and summer rolls.

10. SHISO/PERILLA (*tía tô*) is earthy and bold with peppery, cinnamon and fennel flavours. Often purple on one side and green on the other, it looks like stinging nettles. Also known as Japanese shiso or wild sesame, it is rich in Omega-3 fatty acids, Vitamin A and C, and contains calcium, iron and potassium. Commonly used in China as medicine. Used in salads, summer rolls and cold noodle dishes.

11. BANANA BLOSSOM/FLOWER (*bắp chuối*) is a popular type of vegetable commonly used raw as a crisp garnish or accompaniment to many soups and savoury dishes. It is purchased ready shredded.

12. BETEL LEAVES (*lá lốt*), not to be confused with betel nut chews, have a pungent, minty, peppery taste and smell rather like cinnamon when cooked. The leaves are used as wraps for garlicky beef. Substitute with shiso/perilla leaves.

CORIANDER/CILANTRO (*ngò*) is fragrant, versatile and wonderful. Used liberally as a garnish, or torn over salads. A lot of the flavour is in the stalk.

GARDEN MINT (*rau húng*) is commonly used to add fresh overtones to a dish, especially barbecued vermicelli dishes and zesty soups.

Spices and condiments

1. FRESH GINGER (*gừng*) is considered a medicine or spice. Frequently used for its warm flavour and cleansing effects, it should be in every kitchen. Can be infused in hot water and drunk to aid digestion.

2. COCONUT CARAMEL OR COCONUT SAP SUGAR/HONEY (*nước màu*) is a sweet, smoky coconut caramel used to colour stews and add richness.

3. SÀI GÒN CINNAMON (*quế thanh*) is more like cassia bark than cinnamon. Adds a sweet and intense depth to broths and stews.

4. HOISIN SAUCE (*tương đen*) is a popular condiment for *phở*. It is also great as a central element for dipping sauces for *gỏi cuốn*. Made from soy sauce, soy beans, black beans, molasses and vinegar.

5. OYSTER SAUCE (*dầu hào*) is a Chinese condiment flavoured with oyster extract, great in stir-fries.

6. DEEP-FRIED SHALLOTS (*Hành phi*) are brilliant as a garnish for extra crunch and flavour.

7. CORIANDER SEEDS (*hạt rau mùi*) are used in broths.

8. BLACK PEPPER (*hạt tiêu*) is a common seasoning in broths and other dishes.

9. STAR ANISE (*Đại hồi*) flavours broths (*phở*) and stews. It is one of the traditional Chinese five spices.

10. PREMIUM FISH SAUCE (*nước mắm*) is a staple in Vietnamese cuisine. Made from fermented fish, water and salt, it is imperative to use a good-quality sauce – it will improve the flavour of your cooking immeasurably. Used as a seasoning in cooking as well as in a dipping sauce (*nước chấm*) with cold noodle salads and barbecue meat dishes.

11. SHRIMP PASTE (*mắm ruốc*) is pungent! Made from fermented ground shrimps – good for sauces.

12. DRIED ORANGE PEEL (*vỏ cam khô*) goes in broths, stews and desserts.

13. PEANUTS (*đậu phộng*) – roasted and salted – are chopped and sprinkled over salads, meat dishes, sauces and desserts to add crunch and texture.

14. CHILLI SAUCE (*tương ớt*), eg Sriracha, is made from sun-dried chillies. A common condiment at most dinner tables, it is used in a similar way to ketchup, and added to soups and dips.

15. WOOD EAR MUSHROOMS (*nấm meo*), bought dried and ready shredded, add texture to fillings like in spring rolls.

16. ANNATTO SEEDS (*hột điều màu*) release red colouring when heated in oil, hence are employed to dye broths and stews before being discarded.

17. DRIED CHILLIES (*ớt khô*) are for marinades and seasoning.

18. FRENCH BAKING POWDER (*bột nở Pháp*) has a unique composition that makes it invaluable in making Vietnamese ham and fishcakes.

19. BOUILLON POWDER/SEASONING GRANULES (*hạt nêm*) come in many flavours such as pork, vegetable and mushrooms and are used to season. Similar to stock cubes but in a loose powder.

20. TOASTED SESAME OIL (*dầu mè*) should be used sparingly as seasoning.

21. BLACK CARDAMOM (*thảo quả*) for broth and stews

22. VINEGAR: CIDER, WHITE WINE OR RICE (*giấm*) often replaces lime in dressings with *nước mắm* for sourness. Also used for pickling.

23. MAGGI SEASONING OR SOY SAUCE (*tương*) is a dark, hydrolyzed vegetable protein-based sauce similar to soy sauce but made without soy. Used like soy sauce in cooking and as seasoning at the table.

ROCK SUGAR (*đường phèn*) adds sweetness to soups and desserts. Traditionally produced with cane sugar and honey through slow crystallization. Use a rolling pin to smash it into smaller chunks. Provides a subtly different sweetness to regular sugar, which can be used as a substitute.

SWEETENED CONDENSED MILK (*sữa đặc*) is used in many desserts and also in Vietnamese (iced) coffee.

Rice and noodles

Rice is essential in Vietnamese cuisine – as it is all over South East Asia – providing most of the carbohydrates one would need in a meal. There are different types of rice, and it can be made into noodles. This means that it really comes in all sorts of guises, sizes and shapes to suit the resulting dish: vermicelli salads, rice paper rolls, noodle soups, crêpes, steamed dumplings and doughy buns.

Rice is neutral – neither warming nor cooling for your body – so it can be eaten as often as desired (unless it is fried). This makes for an easy gluten-free diet. However, the Vietnamese have also adopted baguettes and wheat-based noodles in their diets from the French and Chinese and these are perceived as hot ingredients.

Rice is at the core of the Vietnamese diet. It is eaten every day, at least three times, because it is the most filling and satisfying thing you can eat. One would feel a craving for rice (steamed) if it were omitted from meals for more than a couple of days. As long as there is a bowl of rice, everything else falls into place. It can be eaten simply with a few cubes of meat or fish and vegetables or just pickles. If a meal is without rice, it is a snack.

Sometimes, there is nothing more rewarding than rice, fried fish and fish sauce for dipping!

Vietnamese people are seriously strict about their rice and rice products. There are rituals and etiquette: it must be paired correctly, and it belongs in certain dishes and should never be mistakenly placed in the wrong dish. For example, you must never serve rice vermicelli with *phở* and rice in all forms must be cooked to perfection to maintain bite and texture. Some can be eaten at room temperature, like rice vermicelli, and others should be served hot, like *bánh canh* and fresh, flat *phở* noodles.

Noodles are usually one-bowl, one-person meals and not usually served for a big meal or feast for friends and family. Having a stock of dried noodles in the house allows you to throw together simple stir-fries and broths for breakfast, lunch or midnight snacks.

1. **DRIED WHEAT RAMEN** (*mì khô*) is good for rehydrating and adding to broth or pan frying for an instant meal.

2. **RICE FLOUR** (*bột gạo*) is the base for crêpes, dumplings and batter.

3. **SWEET POTATO VERMICELLI** (*miến*), also known as Korean japchae, are silky, chewy and smooth.

4. **THICK RICE VERMICELLI** (*bún*) are best for *huế* noodle soup.

5. **VERY THIN RICE VERMICELLI** (*bánh hỏi*) are light noodles, good for barbecued meat dishes.

6. **FRESH PHỞ NOODLES, ALSO KNOWN AS HO FUN,** (*bánh phở*) are made of rice and used in *phở* and stir-fries.

7. **GLUTINOUS RICE** (*gạo nếp*) is a heavy, sticky rice, perfect for one-bowl meals, especially at breakfast or on journeys.

8. **EGG NOODLES** (*mì*) are Chinese noodles, used in Chinese-inspired noodle soups like won ton soup, or fried noodle dishes.

9. **DRIED, FLAT PHỞ NOODLES** (*hủ tiếu*) are used in *phở*, salads and stews.

10. **RICE VERMICELLI** (*bún*) are common in lots of noodle soups and meat dishes with salad.

11. **BASMATI RICE** (*gạo*) is essential to a meal. Without it, it's not a meal but a snack!

12. **UDON NOODLES** (*bánh canh*) are made of wheat flour and used in soups and stir-fries.

13. **RICE PAPER** (*bánh tráng*) comes in round or square sheets for wrapping up fresh rolls, and sometimes fried spring rolls. Soak in warm water before use.

Awaken the Senses
Breakfast

What to eat for breakfast

Breakfast provides a valuable store of energy for a hard working day. It is usually filled with heat and spice to awaken the senses. After a night's sleep, the body and mind need to be stimulated by hot chilli, warm spices, lively curries and rich hot broth.

Phở and noodle soups such as *bún bò Huế* are a traditional way to fuel the day ahead with plenty of carbohydrates from the noodles. Rejuvenating ginger or lemongrass broths with zingy lime and an array of herbs fire up your motivation for the new day. And if you don't feel like noodle soup, you can have curry or beef stew mopped up with a baguette.

Meat and pickle-filled baguettes are also eaten, spiced up to your liking, or, for those tamer days, a simple fried egg (*bánh mì trứng ốp la*) with soy sauce and a few pieces of soft French cheese "La Vache Qui Rit" to spread on a light, crunchy and fluffy baguette.

People are usually too busy to make breakfast from scratch at home, so it is the norm to eat out at various *phở* street stalls. The rich and poor from all walks of life gather at their favourite noisy stall or store to eat breakfast. But when the soup arrives at the table, silence falls, the ritual begins and then all you can hear is the sucking of noodles and slurping of broth.

Cold breakfasts are rare. If they are eaten, like yogurt and fruit, it is after something hot or warm.

Coffee culture is huge in Vietnam, with rows of cafés full to the brim with men reading newspapers, playing chess or watching the hurried world go by. The most popular drink, iced coffee with condensed milk (*cà phê sữa đá*), is served in a tall glass with an individual filter, or the coffee is drunk hot and neat.

Like all meals, breakfast should be filling without weighing you down.

bánh mì thịt bò nướng xả

Lemongrass beef or pork baguette

Bánh mì is a Vietnamese baguette originally inspired by the French and now a staple in Vietnamese cuisine. It has a light, crunchy exterior and a delicately fluffy inside; some describe biting into one as biting into crispy air.

As with most Vietnamese food, the lightness of the ingredients you fill it with is vital – no one relishes being weighed down. The dough in the centre of the baguette is removed so that you bite straight through the lovely crisp crust to the filling within.

A typical *bánh mì* contains a flavoursome combination of ingredients, the perfect equilibrium of sweet and sour: crunchy carrot and daikon/mooli, a velvety, umami-rich smear of pâté, pieces of BBQ pork, and cooling, fresh coriander/cilantro and cucumber, all dressed with a spicy chilli sauce.

If you cannot buy an authentic Vietnamese baguette, use a regular French baguette.

Lemongrass beef
100 g/3½ oz. beef, thinly sliced
1 lemongrass stalk, finely chopped
1 garlic clove, finely chopped
1 shallot, finely chopped
1 teaspoon Maggi Seasoning (or soy sauce)
1 teaspoon pork, chicken or vegetable bouillon
1 teaspoon sugar

Pickle
2 carrots, shredded
½ daikon/mooli, shredded
5 tablespoons cider vinegar
5 tablespoons sugar

To fill
1 Vietnamese baguette or freshly baked, small French baguette
butter or soft cheese
pork or chicken liver pâté
chả chiên Vietnamese ham, thinly sliced (see page 104 to make your own)
coriander/cilantro
cucumber, cut into 10-cm/ 4-inch slivers
spring onions/scallions, thinly sliced lengthways
Bird's Eye chillies, thinly sliced
Maggi Seasoning
Sriracha chilli sauce

Serves 1

Lemongrass beef
Preheat the oven to 220°C (425°F) Gas 7.

Mix all the ingredients in a bowl and marinate for 10 minutes. Transfer to a roasting pan and bake in the preheated oven for 15 minutes.

Pickle
Mix all the ingredients in a bowl and allow to rest for 15 minutes. Drain and wring with your hands.

To fill
Slit the baguette lengthways and pull out the soft doughy inside (which can be used for breadcrumbs). Spread with butter or soft cheese and a smear of pâté. Layer the warm beef and its juices, pickle, *chả chiên*, coriander/cilantro, cucumber, spring onions/scallions and chillies over the top and squirt over a few drops of Maggi Seasoning and chilli sauce. Enjoy!

A freshly baked baguette, a tasty omelette and an abundance of coriander/cilantro are one of my simplest but greatest pleasures. I love to eat this greedily on a beautiful sunny morning, quietly and alone to absorb the utter goodness! For an extra dimension, drop the sliced chillies into a bowl of good soy sauce and bruise them with the back of a spoon – this releases the chillies' flavour and heat. Drizzle over the baguette.

Omelette baguette
bánh mì trứng ốp lết

Pickle

2 carrots, shredded
½ daikon/mooli, shredded
5 tablespoons cider vinegar
5 tablespoons sugar

Omelette

2 eggs, beaten
2 spring onions/scallions, thinly sliced
½ teaspoon sugar
a pinch of salt
a pinch of black pepper
1 teaspoon soy sauce

1 tablespoon cooking oil
2 Asian shallots, finely chopped

To fill

2 Vietnamese baguettes or freshly baked, small French baguettes
butter
coriander/cilantro
Bird's Eye chillies, thinly sliced (deseeded for less heat)

Serves 2

Pickle

Mix all the ingredients in a bowl and allow to rest for 15 minutes. Drain and wring with your hands.

Omelette

Beat the eggs in a bowl with the spring onions/ scallions, sugar, salt and pepper, and soy sauce.

Heat the oil in a frying pan and briefly fry the shallots. Pour the egg mixture into the pan over the shallots and spread evenly. Cook for a couple of minutes until the underside looks golden brown (lift up one edge and check). Flip the omelette over and cook for a couple of minutes until brown. Remove from the heat and cut into strips.

To fill

Slit the baguette lengthways and pull out the soft doughy inside (which can be used for breadcrumbs). Spread with butter and insert the omelette strips, pickle, coriander/cilantro and chillies.

How to eat pho like
the Vietnamese

Breathe in the beautiful scented broth and taste it, unspoiled by any condiments. Next, squeeze on some lemon or lime juice and add your favoured condiments and garnishes. Mix with chopsticks and a spoon. Pile the ingredients onto your spoon and slurp away, bringing the bowl to your mouth and drinking every last sip of broth.

You can go without most of the garnishes but using the right noodles is very important. It is essential to use *bánh phở* or *hủ tiếu* flat noodles (also called "ho fun"). There should be plenty of noodles in the bowl but these must be submerged in the broth – only the garnishes are placed on top. In Vietnam, you can order extra noodles. Don't forget, this is a breakfast dish – its spicy contents wake you up and the carbohydrates keep you going through the day.

Garnishes of beansprouts, herbs (Thai sweet basil, coriander/cilantro and sawtooth), lime wedges and freshly cut chillies should be served on the side. Never serve the lime wedges already inside the soup. Popular condiments are hoisin sauce and Sriracha chilli sauce.

Whenever I'm in Sài Gòn, I find myself sitting at a kids' table on a red plastic chair, slurping steaming hot beef *phở*. Laced with the warm fragrant spices of star anise, coriander seeds, cinnamon and cloves, with top notes of fresh herbs, onions and citrus and brimming with noodles, every mouthful feels nourishing to the body and mind.

For me, *phở* is about home, wherever that may be. As with most Vietnamese, I constantly crave it, especially when I'm away. Whenever I eat it, I am reminded of the love of my mother and her endless quest to make the perfect *phở* broth. When we first came to England in the early 1980s, it was difficult to find Vietnamese ingredients but the day she discovered where to buy coriander/cilantro, she beamed and made the best pot of *phở* I've ever had.

Beef noodle soup
phở bò

Stock and cooked meat

2 tablespoons sea salt

600 g/1 lb. 5 oz. chopped, boneless oxtail

1.5 kg/3⅓ lbs. beef shin, flank or rib

700 g/1 lb. 9 oz. beef bones/marrow bone

2 litres/8 cups chicken stock

1 large onion, peeled and both ends trimmed

200 g/7 oz. fresh ginger, peeled and halved

1 daikon/mooli, peeled

20 star anise

½ teaspoon cloves

3 cassia bark sticks

2 cinnamon sticks

1 big teaspoon coriander seeds

1 big teaspoon fennel seeds

1 teaspoon black peppercorns

2 black cardamom pods

4 pieces of dried orange peel

3 teaspoons rock salt

50 g/1¾ oz. rock sugar

3 teaspoons pork bouillon

4 tablespoons fish sauce

1 *phở* stock cube (optional)

ground black pepper

Contents

1 red onion, thinly sliced

small handful of coriander/cilantro, finely chopped

2 spring onion/scallions, thinly sliced

4 portions of fresh ho fun noodles, separated and blanched in boiling water; or 2½ packs of flat, dried *phở* noodles (place in a saucepan with a lid, cover with boiling water, add a pinch of salt and a dash of vinegar and apply lid. Leave for 5–10 minutes or according to package instructions. Drain in cold water and separate.)

cooked chicken, torn (optional)

beef fillet, sirloin or rump/round steak, thinly sliced (optional)

Garnishes

Thai sweet basil

coriander/cilantro

sliced Bird's Eye chillies

lime wedges

sawtooth (optional)

beansprouts (optional)

fish sauce

hoisin sauce

Sriracha chilli sauce

chilli oil

very large lidded saucepan muslin/cheesecloth and kitchen twine

Serves 6–8

Stock and cooked meat

Bring a stockpot of water to the boil with the sea salt. Add the meat and bones and boil until scum forms on the surface – about 10 minutes. Remove from the heat and discard the water.

Wash the meat in cold water, removing any scum, and set aside. This will give you a clearer broth.

Meanwhile, wash the pot, add 3 litres/12 cups of fresh water and bring to the boil. Now add the rested meat and bring to a gentle simmer. Skim off any scum and fat from the surface with a spoon. Add the chicken stock. Now heat a stove-top griddle pan over high heat (do not add oil). Char the onion and ginger on both sides. Add to the broth with the daikon/mooli. Put all the spices and the orange peel in a piece of muslin/cheesecloth and tie with twine to seal. Add to the broth with the rock salt and sugar. Simmer for at least 2 hours with the lid on. Check it occasionally and skim off any scum and fat from the surface.

After 2 hours, remove the beef from the pot and allow it to rest slightly, then slice it thinly and store it in a sealed container until serving. Leave the bones and oxtail in the pot and simmer for at least 1 hour.

After 1 hour, add the pork bouillon, fish sauce, *phở* stock cube and black pepper, to taste.

Contents

Mix together the red onion, coriander/cilantro and spring onions/scallions. Place 1 portion of cooked noodles into a big, deep soup bowl with a pinch of black pepper. Place the cooked beef and chicken, if using, on top and sprinkle with the red-onion mixture. To make it special, add raw beef (it will cook perfectly with the hot broth). Bring the broth to boiling point, then pour ladles of it over the noodles to submerge them.

Garnishes

Serve the garnishes and condiments on the side and add them to your *phở* as desired.

My grandmother was a great entrepreneur; in order to support her family, she opened up her front room to sell *bún bò huế*, the best noodle soup I have ever eaten. It originates from Huế (the city of temples, emperor's palaces and dynasties in central Vietnam) and is spicy, bold and invigorating.

Hue noodle soup with beef and pork
bún bò huế

Stock and cooked meat

2 tablespoons salt
1 kg/2¼ lbs. rib of beef
500 g/1 lb. beef shin/flank
600 g/1 lb. 5 oz. chopped, boneless oxtail
2 pig's trotters (optional)
2 litres/8 cups chicken stock
1 large onion, peeled and both ends trimmed
6 lemongrass stalks, bashed
40 g/1½ oz. rock sugar
1 daikon/mooli, peeled
1 tablespoon salt
1 tablespoon shrimp paste
1 tablespoon pork bouillon
1 *bún bò huế* stock cube (optional)
4 tablespoons fish sauce
3 tablespoons cooking oil
½ bulb of garlic, cloves separated, peeled and finely chopped
2 lemongrass stalks, finely diced
½ teaspoon chilli powder
½ tablespoon annatto powder

Contents

2 spring onion/scallions, thinly sliced
½ red onion, thinly sliced
8 sprigs of coriander/ cilantro, roughly chopped (stalk on)
450 g/1 lb. thick rice vermicelli (place in a saucepan with a lid, cover with boiling water and apply lid. Leave for 20 minutes or according to package instructions. Drain and rinse with hot water.)
chả chiên Vietnamese ham, thinly sliced (see page 104 to make your own)
leaves from 8 sprigs of hot mint (optional)

Garnishes

lime wedges
Thai sweet basil
sliced Bird's Eye chillies
beansprouts
banana blossom (optional)
curly morning glory (optional)
cockscomb mint (optional)
shiso/perilla (optional)

very large lidded saucepan
muslin/cheesecloth and kitchen twine

Serves 6–8

Stock and cooked meat

Following the instructions on page 26, boil all the meat together for 10 minutes, then wash it and rest it.

Wash the pot, add 3 litres/12 cups of fresh water and bring to the boil. Now add the rested meat and bring to a gentle simmer. Skim off any scum and fat from the surface with a spoon. Add the chicken stock. Now heat a stove-top griddle pan over high heat (do not add oil). Char the onion and 6 lemongrass stalks on both sides. Add to the broth with the sugar, daikon/mooli and salt. Simmer for at least 2 hours with the lid on. Check it occasionally and skim off any scum and fat from the surface.

After 2 hours, remove the beef from the pot and allow it to rest slightly, then slice it thinly and store it in a sealed container until serving. Add the shrimp paste, pork bouillon, stock cube, if using, and fish sauce to the broth. In another pan, heat the oil and fry the garlic, diced lemongrass and chilli powder. Add to the broth with the annatto powder and simmer.

Contents

Mix the onions and coriander/cilantro. Put a serving of vermicelli in a big, deep soup bowl. Put the cooked beef on top and sprinkle with the red-onion mixture and mint, if using. Bring the broth to boiling point and pour enough over the vermicelli to submerge them.

Garnishes

Squeeze lime into the soup. Serve the other garnishes on the side and add them to your *huế* as desired.

Vietnamese curry is fragrant, light and mild, eaten with baguette to kickstart your day. It is more like a stew with chicken, carrots and potato and lots of lemongrass and coconut curry broth to dip your bread in. You can add more heat and other vegetables to your liking. When I was little, my mother so cleverly saved money and time by cooking a delicious and nutritious meal in one pot. When we couldn't get baguette, she made white bread toast and butter for us to dip in – it's still one of my most favourite things today.

Chicken curry
cà ri gà

1 tablespoon cooking oil
1 red onion, roughly chopped
1 thumb's worth of fresh ginger, finely chopped
1 lemongrass stalk, finely diced
2 large chicken legs, cut into bite-size pieces, or 6 whole drumsticks, skin on
3 teaspoons curry powder
2 garlic cloves, finely chopped
165 ml/⅔ cup coconut milk
300 ml/1¼ cups chicken stock
2 medium potatoes, cubed
1 carrot, roughly sliced
4 tablespoons fish sauce

1 teaspoon sugar
ground black pepper
½ aubergine/eggplant, cubed (optional)
handful of okra, cut into bite-size pieces (optional)
6 Asian shallots, peeled
handful of mangetout/snow peas (optional)
warm baguette and butter, or steamed rice, to serve

Garnishes (all chopped)
Thai sweet basil
spring onion/scallion
Bird's Eye chillies

Serves 2

Heat the oil in a medium saucepan over low heat. Gently fry the red onion, ginger and lemongrass. Once the onion has softened, add the chicken legs and fry, turning often, until they're evenly browned.

Add the curry powder, stirring well until the chicken legs are well coated. Add the garlic, coconut milk, chicken stock, potatoes and carrot and stir. Cover with a lid and simmer for about 10 minutes.

Season the curry with the fish sauce, sugar and a pinch of black pepper, then add the aubergine/eggplant, okra, shallots and mangetout/snow peas. Cook for a further 8–10 minutes, or until the chicken is cooked through.

Garnishes
Garnish with Thai sweet basil, spring onion/scallion and chillies. Serve with a fresh, warm baguette and butter, or a bowl of steamed rice.

Lemongrass and star anise perfume the air when this is stewing on the stove, making any place feel like home. The ultimate comfort food, *bò kho* is spicy and fragrant enough to awaken the senses at the start of the day. It is a thrifty dish designed to make use of cheap cuts of beef and whichever vegetables you have that need to be used up – my mother loves the simplicity of carrot, potatoes and peas.

Beef stew with star anise
bò kho

Stew
2 tablespoons cooking oil
1 teaspoon annatto seeds
1 onion, roughly chopped
450 g/1 lb. braising beef, beef tendons or rib, cubed
2 teaspoons dried chilli flakes/dried hot pepper flakes
1 teaspoon ground cumin
10 star anise
1 bay leaf
1 teaspoon paprika
½ teaspoon ground cloves
2 garlic cloves, sliced
2-cm/1-inch piece of fresh ginger, coarsely chopped
2 lemongrass stalks (outer layer removed), finely chopped
400 ml/1⅔ cups cider (or coconut water, but halve the sugar)
100 ml/⅓ cup chicken or beef stock

2 carrots, roughly sliced
2 medium potatoes, cubed
2 teaspoons sugar
3 tablespoons fish sauce
1 teaspoon cornflour/cornstarch
130 g/1 cup fresh or frozen peas
ground black pepper
280 g/10 oz. thick rice vermicelli, cooked, or warm baguette and butter (buttered toast also works)

Garnishes (optional)
lime wedges
beansprouts
Thai sweet basil
garden mint
coriander/cilantro
sawtooth

Serves 4

Heat the oil in a large saucepan over medium heat. Fry the annatto seeds for a couple of minutes until the reddish colour is released. Pour the oil into a bowl and discard the seeds.

In the same pan over low heat, gently fry the onion until softened. Turn the heat up to high and add the beef. Fry it, turning it often, until browned all over. You may need to do this in batches – if the meat is too cramped, it will stew rather than sear properly.

Add the chilli/pepper flakes, cumin, star anise, bay leaf, paprika, cloves, garlic, ginger and lemongrass and pour in the cider, stock and reserved red annatto oil. Stir well. Cover the pan with the lid and cook for about 15 minutes.

Add the carrots and potatoes and season with the sugar and fish sauce. Reduce the heat to low–medium and cook with the lid on for a further 30 minutes.

Put the cornflour/cornstarch and a few drops of water in a small bowl and stir to mix. Add it to the stew, along with the peas, and cook for 5–10 minutes, stirring occasionally, until the sauce has thickened slightly. The beef should be tender, but the cooking time may vary so braise it for longer if it is still tough. Season with more fish sauce or pepper, to taste, and remove the star anise. Serve with the vermicelli.

Garnishes
Squeeze lime into the stew. Serve the other garnishes on the side.

My mum makes the best version of this in the world! It is great to take on journeys, as it remains moist and sticky in its box or banana leaf and can be consumed hot or cold. Whole train journeys can be spent snacking on fruit, *bánh mì* and sticky rice. Every Vietnamese I've met carries food on journeys from one region to another, to ease hunger as well as to gift to loved ones.

Sticky rice with Chinese sausage
xôi lạp xưởng

400 g/2¼ cups glutinous
    rice
about 3 tablespoons dried
    shiitake mushrooms
3 tablespoons dried
    shrimps
dash of cooking oil
3 Asian shallots, chopped
1 spring onion/scallion,
    thinly sliced
1 *lạp xưởng* Chinese
    sausage (45 g/1½ oz.),
    thinly sliced (if you
    really can't find it, use
    Italian cured sausage)
a pinch of sea salt
a pinch of black pepper
½ teaspoon sugar
a pinch of pork or
    vegetable bouillon

To serve
sliced spring onion/
    scallion
pickled shallots and
    lotus roots
chà chiên Vietnamese ham,
    thinly sliced (see page
    104 to make your own)

steamer

Serves 4

You will need to start soaking some of the ingredients 1 hour before you begin cooking. Put the rice in a bowl, cover with warm water and allow to soak for 1 hour. Put the shiitake mushrooms in a bowl, cover with warm water and allow to soak for 20–30 minutes or until soft. Put the dried shrimps in a bowl, cover with warm water and allow to soak for 10 minutes. When ready, drain the rice, shiitake mushrooms and shrimps and pat them all dry.

Heat the oil in a frying pan over medium heat and fry the shallots and spring onion/scallion until softened. Add the sausage, shrimps and mushrooms and fry for 5 minutes. Add this to the rice in a large bowl with the salt, pepper, sugar and bouillon and mix.

Get the steamer ready with simmering water. Put the rice mixture in the steamer in a ring shape to allow the steam to rise through the middle. Steam for 30–40 minutes on medium heat, stirring every 10 minutes so that everything cooks evenly. Check there is enough water in the base.

Remove from the heat and allow to steam for 10 minutes.

To serve
Serve hot with spring onion/scallion, pickles and ham. You can also steam the rice in banana-leaf parcels; re-steam them to reheat, if needed.

Feed
the Soul
Soups

Canh chua is one of my favourite dinnertime soups, always best when my mother makes it and we enjoy it together with some steamed rice. It's a sweet, sour and hot fish soup. It doesn't take long to cook, which means the vegetables stay whole and crunchy. It always reminds me of my mum's happy face, the sunshine and being in Vietnam, when the whole family sit together on the floor with a spread of dishes to share.

Hot and sour fish soup
canh chua cá

3 tablespoons cooking oil
1 whole sea bass (300 g/
    10½ oz.), scaled, gutted
    and cut in half
    widthways (keep the
    head, for flavour)
2 Asian shallots, finely
    chopped
2 garlic cloves, finely
    chopped
2 tomatoes, quartered
120 g/4 oz. canned
    pineapple rings, cubed
1 teaspoon sugar
2 tablespoons fish sauce
1 spring onion/scallion,
    cut into 2-cm/1-inch
    pieces
freshly squeezed juice of
    1 lime
60 g/1 cup beansprouts
1 Bird's Eye chilli, thinly
    sliced on the diagonal

20-cm/8-inch stick of taro
    stem/elephant ear (*bạc
    hà*), peeled and thinly
    sliced (optional)
steamed rice or rice
    vermicelli, to serve

Chilli-fish sauce
1 Bird's Eye chilli
3 tablespoons fish sauce

Garnishes (all chopped)
garden mint
coriander/cilantro,
    stalk on
sawtooth, Thai sweet basil
    or rice paddy herb
    (optional)

Serves 2

This dish is all about preparation. Make sure everything is cut and prepped beforehand because hardly any time is spent cooking.

Heat 1 tablespoon of the oil in a frying pan over medium heat and fry the sea bass for 4 minutes on each side. Remove from the pan and set aside.

In the same pan, add 1 tablespoon of the oil and gently fry the shallots and garlic until soft. Set aside.

Bring 600 ml/2½ cups water to the boil in a large saucepan, then add the reserved fish head, tomatoes, pineapple, sugar, fish sauce and seared fish. Bring to the boil again and boil for 2 minutes.

Add the spring onion/scallion, lime juice, remaining oil and the shallots and garlic. Turn off the heat.

Chilli-fish sauce
Drop the whole chilli into a serving dish (large enough to hold the fish pieces) and add the fish sauce. Bruise the chilli with the back of a spoon to release the chilli's flavour and heat. Transfer the fish pieces to this dish.

Put the beansprouts, sliced chilli and taro stem/elephant ear in a large serving bowl. Pour the soup in. Serve with the fish, and steamed rice or rice vermicelli.

Garnishes
Sprinkle the garnishes over the soup and you have a palate-cleansing sweet and sour soup with a dish of poached fish.

Mustard greens and tofu broth
canh cải bẹ xanh
đậu phụ gừng

100 g/1 cup cubed fresh tofu
2-cm/1-inch piece of fresh ginger, julienned
1 spring onion/scallion, thinly sliced
1 vegetable stock cube
dash of cooking oil
a pinch of sea salt
a pinch of black pepper
a pinch of sugar
300 g/10½ oz. Chinese mustard greens, chopped

Serves 2 as a main/entrée, and up to 6 as part of a meal of many sharing dishes

Bring 1 litre/4 cups water to the boil in a saucepan. Add the tofu, ginger, spring onion/scallion, stock cube, oil, salt, pepper and sugar.

When you are ready to serve the soup, add the Chinese mustard greens to the pan and bring to the boil again.

Serve hot by itself as a main meal or with an array of other dishes and rice.

Alternatively, you can add spinach, watercress, bok choy or choi sum instead of Chinese mustard greens. It is also absolutely irresistible as a noodle soup base. Just add a portion of dried ramen or fresh udon noodles and cook for 2–3 minutes.

This is a great palate-cleansing soup to be had with an array of dishes at lunch or dinner with family or a few friends. The leaves can be consumed at any time and the refreshing broth can be slurped from your bowl in between rice servings. Sometimes it is great to add ramen to the broth for a midnight snack.

In Phan Thiết where my mother comes from, the street vendors sell this as a night meal. It is among one of my favourite noodle soups. In this recipe, the chicken-stock broth is flavoured by the fishcakes and fried shallots. Dill, mint and lime brings it together to make it the most enticing yet cleansing thing to eat when the moon shines. This is a very versatile soup, so the broth can be made from any stock, and you can use fish fillets, seafood such as prawns/shrimp, crab and squid, and meat such as chicken and pork.

Udon noodle soup with fishcakes
bánh canh cá thác lác thìa là

Fishcakes with Dill (page 100), uncooked
3 tablespoons cooking oil
2 litres/8 cups chicken, pork or vegetable stock
½ teaspoon coarsely ground black pepper
2 teaspoons sugar
2 teaspoons sea salt
1 teaspoon pork bouillon or 1 chicken stock cube (optional)
2 tablespoons fish sauce
800 g/1¾ lbs. fresh udon noodles
2 tablespoons cooking oil
8 Asian shallots, chopped

Garnishes
storebought deep-fried shallots (optional)
garden mint, chopped
coriander/cilantro, coarsely chopped
garlic chives, cut into 2-cm/1-inch pieces (optional)
dill, finely chopped (optional)
cockscomb mint, torn (optional)
sliced Bird's Eye chillies
lime wedges

Serves 4

Take two-thirds of the uncooked fishcake mixture and shape into a patty. Heat 1 tablespoon of the oil in a frying pan and fry the patty on both sides until golden. Cut it into thin slices.

Pinch off bite-size pieces from the remaining uncooked fishcake mixture and roll into rough balls. Set aside.

Put the stock, pepper, sugar, salt, pork bouillon and fish sauce in a saucepan over medium heat and bring to a gentle boil.

Meanwhile, heat 2 tablespoons of the oil in a frying pan and fry the shallots until brown and crispy.

Bring another pan of water to the boil and blanch the noodles for 2 minutes. Drain and divide them between 4 soup bowls. Add the slices of fried fishcake and a generous pinch of the chopped herbs from the garnishes. Add more pepper, to taste.

When ready to serve, make sure the pan of broth is still boiling, then add the uncooked fish balls. After a couple of minutes when they have floated to the surface, tip in your fried shallots. Ladle the soup into the prepared soup bowls.

Garnishes
Scatter the remaining herbs, the deep-fried shallots and chillies over the soup and serve with the lime.

cháo vịt

Cháo is the transformation of small amounts of rice: after prolonged simmering in broth, it turns into a thick porridge soup. This is a great way to use up leftover cooked rice or when you do not have much rice going, as you can make it go a long way. However, this basic dish can be lifted into something much more luxurious by cooking the *cháo* with duck as a great treat for visitors. It is then served with slices of duck next to the congee and alongside a ginger-based *nước chấm* dipping sauce. If you prefer, you can use a whole chicken instead of duck. To make life easier, ask the butcher to joint the duck and poach it in pieces instead of whole. Or use chicken stock instead of water and poach pre-cut chicken or duck breast for 30 minutes in the congee broth.

Duck congee

1.5-kg/3¼-lb. whole duck
1 big tablespoon salt
200 g/1¼ cups basmati rice, rinsed
1 teaspoon sugar
1 thumb's worth of fresh ginger, finely chopped
1 teaspoon pork bouillon (optional)
a pinch of black pepper

Onion pickle
1 red onion, thinly sliced
3 tablespoons cider vinegar
½ teaspoon black pepper
1 tablespoon sugar

Dipping sauce
2 garlic cloves, crushed
1 thumb's worth of fresh ginger, finely chopped
2 Bird's Eye chillies, thinly sliced
3 tablespoons cider vinegar
3 tablespoons sugar
4 tablespoons fish sauce

Garnishes (all chopped)
garden or hot mint
coriander/cilantro
Thai sweet basil
spring onions/scallions
limes
fresh ginger

Serves 6–8

Bring 2 litres/8 cups water to the boil in a very large saucepan over medium heat. Add the whole duck and the salt and bring back to the boil. Add the rice, sugar, ginger, bouillon and pepper. Cover the pan with the lid and simmer for 75–90 minutes over low heat.

Onion pickle
Combine the ingredients and leave for at least 1 hour.

Dipping sauce
Combine the garlic, ginger, chillies and vinegar and leave for about 5 minutes – the vinegar will slightly "cook" the ingredients. Add the sugar and fish sauce. Divide between individual dipping bowls and leave for at least 1 hour.

Remove the pan from the heat, take the duck out and set it aside to rest and cool slightly. Now joint the duck, slice the flesh and arrange it on a serving dish.

Divide the hot congee between 6–8 soup bowls. Serve with the duck, onion pickle and dipping sauce.

Garnishes
Serve the garnishes with the congee and duck.

Yin and yang

Since we were children, my mother has brought us up on a basic philosophy of yin and yang, a principle that shapes everything in the universe, including our health: there are two sides to everything, what goes up must come down, what goes in must come out, and therefore how and what we eat bear consequences on our bodies and minds.

The Vietnamese diet is very much based on the general rules of yin and yang. Everything has yin (cold) and yang (hot) aspects to it. Ingredients are either hot, warm, neutral or cold and thereby affect the body and soul, having the potential to make it balanced, too heated or too cool.

In a meal, different varieties of ingredients are combined to create a harmony of taste and texture as well as of yin and yang. The two elements complement each other and work in unison, with rice products playing an essential role in the neutral middle. Red meat, onion, root vegetables and exotic fruits grown and ripened in high sun are very hot for the body, as are deep-fried foods. Fish and chicken are warming. Green and leafy vegetables, melon and other fruits are cooling.

For thousands of years, this principle has been upheld and food has been treated as medicine. By paying attention to and understanding how our bodies respond to food, the right choices can be made for health, wellbeing and longevity.

Naturally "hot" people tend to have restless nights, be thirsty, have headaches, nose bleeds, be irritated, impatient and so on and therefore have to eat more cooling foods, like leafy vegetables.

"Cool" people tend to be tired, low in spirits, with a slow metabolism and therefore should eat beef dishes and root vegetables.

Understanding how food affects and heals us is a lesson passed down from generation to generation.

This quick, light, refreshing, sweet and tangy soup can be eaten day or night. The base is simple enough to embrace any herbs and extras such as fried tofu, fishcakes, ham and blood cakes. My mother often made it when we were growing up; she said it reminded her of her home town by the seaside and her brothers and sisters. As a young mother with two children to raise, this was a delicious budget meal as it works well with canned crabmeat.

Crab, tomato and omelette soup
bún riêu cua

4 tablespoons dried
   shrimps
2 litres/8 cups chicken,
   vegetable or pork stock
4 tomatoes, quartered
freshly squeezed juice of
   ½ lemon or lime
2 tablespoons sugar
3 tablespoons fish sauce
1 teaspoon shrimp paste
240 g/8½ oz. canned
   (lump) crabmeat,
   squeezed of excess
   moisture
4 eggs
a pinch of sea salt
a pinch of black pepper
a pinch of sugar
1 teaspoon cooking oil
2 Asian shallots, thinly
   sliced
cooked rice vermicelli,
   to serve

Optional fillings
1 quantity Fishcakes with
   Dill (page 100), sliced
chả chiên Vietnamese
   ham, thinly sliced (see
   page 104 to make your
   own)

Garnishes (optional)
lime wedges
sliced Bird's Eye chillies
garden mint
hot mint
cockscomb mint
shiso/perilla leaves
Thai sweet basil
coriander/cilantro
banana blossom
curly morning glory
beansprouts

Serves 4

Put the dried shrimps in a bowl, cover with warm water and allow to soak for 10 minutes. Drain and pat dry.

Put the stock, shrimps and tomatoes in a large saucepan over high heat and bring to the boil. Season with the lemon or lime juice, sugar, fish sauce and shrimp paste, then reduce to a medium heat.

Put the crabmeat, eggs, salt, pepper and sugar in a bowl and beat with a fork until well mixed.

Bring the broth back to a gentle boil. Create a whirlpool in the broth by stirring it around quickly, then pour the egg mixture into the middle. Stop stirring once all the mixture is in. It will rise to the top and form a floating omelette.

Meanwhile, put the oil in a frying pan and fry the shallots until golden.

When ready to serve, make sure the pan of broth is still boiling, then break up any large pieces of omelette and add the browned shallots.

Optional fillings
Put the fishcake slices, ham and cooked rice vermicelli in 4 bowls and pour the broth over the top.

Garnishes
Serve the garnishes on the side.

This quicker and easier version of *cháo* is ideal when you are feeling under the clouds. It is light, cleansing and easily digestible. My mother usually makes me eat this if I am suffering from a cold. When you are ill, she says, your body has to do a lot to heal; it shouldn't have to work hard to digest. This *cháo* helps to heat up the body with the goodness of ginger and fish and fades away easily with its lightness.

Fish congee with ginger
cháo cá gừng

100 g/1 cup cooked basmati rice
1 whole sea bass, seabream, salmon or trout (250 g/9 oz.), scaled, gutted and filleted (keep the carcass)
1 tablespoon cooking oil
a pinch of sea salt
a pinch of black pepper
a pinch of sugar
1 tablespoon fish sauce
1 thumb's worth of fresh ginger, finely chopped

Garnishes
sliced spring onion/ scallion
coriander/cilantro
sliced Bird's Eye chilli
lime wedges

Serves 2

Put 750 ml/3 cups water and the cooked rice in a large saucepan over medium heat and bring to the boil. Add the reserved fish carcass and boil for 20 minutes. Skim off any scum from the surface with a spoon.

Meanwhile, heat the oil in a frying pan over high heat and fry the fish fillets, skin side down, for a couple of minutes to brown and cook through. Set aside.

Remove the carcass from the broth. Season with the salt, pepper, sugar and fish sauce and add the ginger. Cook for 5 minutes.

Divide the broth and fish between 2 soup bowls.

Garnishes
Serve with the garnishes on the side.

7. Sticky Fingers
Snacks

The French made a distinctive mark on Vietnamese cuisine and this light puffy snack is one streetfood example. My mother has been making them since she discovered ready-made puff pastry at the supermarket and I sometimes fill them with chicken curry or beef stew! The Vietnamese enjoy pastry snacks like these often.

Puff pastry chicken pies
bánh patê sô gà nấm và đậu hòa lan

100 g/3½ oz. skinless
  chicken breast
1 teaspoon cooking oil
2 tablespoons butter
3 garlic cloves, finely
  chopped
2 chestnut mushrooms,
  finely chopped
50 g/⅓ cup garden peas
1 teaspoon pork bouillon
1 teaspoon sugar
½ teaspoon black pepper
1 tablespoon tapioca
  starch
320 g/11 oz. ready-rolled
  puff pastry dough,
  thawed if frozen
1 egg yolk, lightly beaten
Sriracha chilli sauce,
  to serve

6-cm/2½-inch round
  cookie cutter or glass
baking sheet, greased

Makes 6

Chop the chicken into 1-cm/½-inch cubes or quickly pulse into pieces in a food processor.

Heat the oil in a saucepan over medium heat, then add the chicken, butter, garlic, mushrooms, peas, pork bouillon, sugar and pepper. Fry until the chicken is golden.

Put the tapioca starch and 5 tablespoons water in a bowl and stir together. Pour into the pan and stir well. This will thicken and bind everything together. Cook for 1 minute, then remove from the heat and allow to rest while you prepare the pastry.

Preheat the oven to 180°C (350°F) Gas 4.

Unroll the puff pastry dough on a lightly floured surface. Use the cookie cutter or upturned glass to stamp out 12 rounds from the dough. Brush egg yolk over all the rounds with a pastry brush. Put each pastry round on your hand and put a generous tablespoon of fried and cooled filling in the centre. Place on the prepared baking sheet, top with the remaining rounds and press the tines of a fork all around the edges to seal the 2 pastry rounds together.

Bake the pies in the preheated oven for about 35 minutes or until golden. Serve immediately, with chilli sauce.

When we first came to London, this was the easiest thing for my mother to make, as most of the ingredients were available from Chinatown. She got everyone she came across, from teachers and neighbours to priests, to fall in love with our family thanks to her spring rolls. They are traditionally eaten hot with herbs wrapped around them and dipped into *nước chấm* sauce.

Spring rolls
chả giò

about 24 fresh square spring roll pastry wrappers, about 14 cm/ 5½ inches, thawed if frozen

up to 3 litres/3 quarts sunflower or vegetable oil

Filling

3 tablespoons dried shredded wood ear mushrooms

50 g/1¾ oz. glass (cellophane) noodles

250 g/9 oz. minced/ ground chicken or pork

175 g/6 oz. king prawns/ jumbo shrimp, shelled, deveined and coarsely chopped

120 g/4 oz. canned (lump) crabmeat, squeezed of excess moisture

250 g/9 oz. white yam, peeled and julienned

2 carrots, shredded

120 g/2 cups beansprouts

1 tablespoon sugar

1 tablespoon pork bouillon

a pinch of coarse black pepper

a pinch of sea salt

2 spring onions/scallions, thinly sliced

2 garlic cloves, finely chopped

Dipping sauce and garnishes

2 Bird's Eye chillies, finely chopped

2 garlic cloves, finely chopped

2 tablespoons cider vinegar

2 tablespoons fish sauce

2 tablespoons sugar

lettuce leaves

Thai sweet basil

coriander/cilantro

hot mint

deep fat fryer (optional)

Makes about 24

Filling

Put the wood ear mushrooms in a bowl, cover with warm water and allow to soak for at least 30 minutes. When ready, drain the mushrooms and pat them dry.

Cook the noodles according to the instructions on the package. Drain, pat dry and cut into short lengths.

When you are ready to assemble the rolls, make sure all the filling ingredients are prepared, dry and mixed together. Start to heat up your deep fat fryer, or a large, deep pan half-filled with oil over medium heat. Heat the oil to 140°C/285°F or until a cube of bread dropped in sizzles and browns in 1 minute.

Place a pastry wrapper diagonally in front of you. Spoon 1 tablespoon of the filling towards the lower corner. Fold the 2 side corners inward over the filling, as if making an envelope, then fold the bottom corner over. Roll up the package tightly, tucking in the filling in a neat cylinder as you roll it towards the far corner. Seal the flap with a touch of oil. Deep fry the roll for 4–5 minutes until golden. Remove and drain on a kitchen paper/paper towel, taste, then adjust the seasoning of the remaining filling if needed. Now assemble and deep fry the remaining rolls in batches.

Dipping sauce and garnishes

Mix together the garlic, chillies and vinegar in a bowl. Set aside for 2 minutes. This "cooks" the garlic. Now add the fish sauce, sugar and 400 ml/1½ cups water.

Wrap each roll in a lettuce leaf with herbs and serve with the dipping sauce in individual bowls.

This traditional recipe is from Sài Gòn but every region has its own take on fresh summer rolls. Although they are great for special occasions, they are tasty and healthy enough to take to work for lunch – you'll be enjoying a good herb and prawn salad inside rice paper.

Sai Gon fresh summer rolls
gỏi cuốn sai gon

6 rice paper sheets, about 22 cm/9 inches

Filling
150 g/5½ oz. pork belly
18 king prawns/jumbo shrimp, shelled and deveined
30 g/1 oz. rice vermicelli
6 lettuce leaves
12 coriander/cilantro sprigs, stalk on, chopped
18 garden or hot mint leaves, chopped
3 cockscomb mint sprigs
18 shiso/perilla leaves
6 garlic chives, halved and head removed

Dipping sauce
1 tablespoon cooking oil
1 garlic clove, chopped
2 tablespoons hoisin sauce
½ tablespoon white wine vinegar or cider vinegar
1 teaspoon sugar
½ tablespoon Sriracha chilli sauce
2 tablespoons roasted salted peanuts, crushed

Makes 6

Filling
Bring a saucepan of water and a few pinches of salt to the boil. Add the pork, cover with a lid and cook for 15 minutes or until the juices run clear when you prick it with a knife. Allow to cool, then cut off the skin and very thinly slice the meat.

Put the prawns/shrimp and a pinch of salt in a saucepan of boiling water and poach for 2 minutes, or until opaque. Drain and allow to cool.

Put the rice vermicelli, a pinch of salt and a dash of vinegar in a bowl or pan of boiling water, cover and allow to cook for 5–10 minutes or until soft. Drain and rinse with hot water.

Once the pork, prawns/shrimp and vermicelli are ready, put them and the remaining filling ingredients in their own individual bowls in front of you. Pour some warm water into a tray deep and large enough to submerge the rice paper sheets. Use a plastic board as a base on which to make the rolls.

Dip a sheet of rice paper into the water and take it out as soon as it is moist all over – do not let it sit in the water. Lay the sheet on the plastic board. Imagine the sheet is a face and now place the filling where the mouth should be: line up a couple of pork slices, 3 prawns/shrimp, 1 lettuce leaf, and one-sixth of the vermicelli and herbs. Fold the 2 sides inward over the filling, as if you were making an envelope. Now fold the bottom corner over the filling. Put 3–4 pieces of garlic chives along the roll with the tips sticking out of one end of the roll. Start to roll up the package tightly, pushing it forward and tucking in the filling in a neat cylinder as you roll it towards the far side of the sheet. Keep in an airtight container or wrap in clingfilm/plastic wrap while you assemble the remaining summer rolls.

Dipping sauce
Heat the oil in a saucepan over medium heat. Fry the garlic until it browns slightly. Add the hoisin sauce, vinegar, sugar, chilli sauce and 1 tablespoon water and bring to a gentle boil. Pour into dipping bowls and sprinkle the peanuts on top. Serve with the rolls for dipping.

My mother never follows recipes; she throws in a bit of this and that and relies on her taste buds to get the right balance of sweet, sour, salty and hot. Every time she makes this, my brother and I eat every last grain and morsel.

Chicken salad with hot mint
gà xé phay và rau răm

Onion pickle

1 red onion, thinly sliced

3 tablespoons cider vinegar

1 tablespoon sugar

a pinch of sea salt

a pinch of black pepper

Salad

3 chicken thighs, skin on and bone in

1 chicken stock cube

200 g/1¼ cups basmati rice

1 knob of butter

1 garlic clove, finely chopped

10 hot mint sprigs (or Thai sweet basil), chopped

a small handful of coriander/cilantro, stalk on, chopped

a pinch of black pepper

Dipping sauce

2 tablespoons fish sauce

2 teaspoons sugar

2-cm/1-inch piece of fresh ginger, finely chopped

1 Bird's Eye chilli, finely chopped

1 garlic clove, finely chopped

1 tablespoon cider vinegar

Serves 2–3

Onion pickle

Set aside about one-fifth of the onion slices. Combine the remainder with the other ingredients and leave for at least 1 hour.

Salad

Put 1.2 litres/5 cups cold water and the chicken thighs in a saucepan over medium heat and cover with a lid. Bring to the boil, then skim off the scum from the surface with a spoon. Add the stock cube and cook for 25–30 minutes (but you will need to extract some of the stock 20 minutes into cooking – see below).

Wash and drain the rice. Finely chop the reserved portion of red onion. Melt the butter in a non-stick saucepan over low heat and fry the onion and garlic. Add the rice and stir it to coat it in the flavours. Once the chicken has been poaching in the other pan for 20 minutes, take out 350 ml/1½ cups of the poaching stock and pour it into the pan of rice with a pinch of salt. Cover with a lid and raise the heat to medium; this technique will cook the rice beautifully by steaming it. When the liquid comes to the boil, turn the heat back down to low and continue to cook for 15–20 minutes, stirring occasionally.

Dipping sauce

Mix the ingredients together in a bowl with 2 tablespoons of the leftover chicken poaching stock.

When the chicken has finished poaching, remove it from the pan and allow it to rest for 10 minutes while the rice is still cooking. Reserve the leftover stock for another time – allow it to cool completely, then refrigerate or freeze it.

Tear the meat from the chicken bones using your fingers or 2 forks. Discard the skin. Mix the chicken with the onion pickle (discarding the pickling juices), mint, coriander/cilantro and pepper.

Serve the salad at room temperature with the rice and dipping sauce.

Streetfood

In Vietnam, the best food comes from the street, where you can buy *bánh mì* (meat- and herb-filled baguettes), *chè* (all kinds of desserts), *bánh* (sweet and savoury cakes/buns), fried bananas and soups – almost anything you would want to eat.

The food is homemade, generally by the vendor who usually specializes in the one thing he or she is selling. And he does it well, because the Saigonese are fussy and want everything fresh, done in a certain way.

People use the street to sell food in carts, baskets, markets – even living rooms can be opened up to the street to be turned into eateries. Teenagers walk around drumming beats with a spoon on an icebreaker to announce home deliveries. There is an allotted time for street snacks: crêpes in the evening, banana fritters in the afternoon and so on, with seasonal fruits available at all times. The smell of baked coconut custard buns and barbecued meat is enough to entice any hungry passer-by.

For city dwellers, life resides on sidewalks. People love to open their entire living rooms to the street and invite friends and neighbours to squat and chat over a refreshing drink or snack, and to play with children, if only to get a breeze from the heat and humidity that lives through the seasons. The front door is an unfenced window, exposed to the heart and soul of the neighbourhood, where there is always hunger or the anticipation of hunger.

Today, many people can live without ever needing to cook at home, as what they buy on the street from a favourite vendor is generally cooked at home. Many dishes can be time consuming and expensive to make on a small scale, so it can be easier to buy it ready made and it will always come with all the right garnishes and dipping sauces.

This is my take on my favourite British dish, fish and chips. It got everyone in London talking about my supper club. You can use salmon, too.

Raw fish and chips
cá ngừ sống và khoai tây chiên

Fish

2 teaspoons soy sauce

1-cm/½-inch piece of ginger, finely chopped

4 tablespoons orange juice

1 teaspoon wasabi paste

1 spring onion/scallion, thinly sliced

200 g/7-oz. line-caught, sashimi-grade tuna

Chips

1–2 litres/4–8 cups vegetable oil

400 g/14 oz. Maris Piper/russet potatoes, cut into fat matchsticks

sea salt

Wasabi mayo

7 tablespoons mayonnaise

1 teaspoon wasabi paste

deep fat fryer (optional)

Serves 2

Fish

Combine the soy sauce, ginger, orange juice and wasabi in a bowl. With a sharp knife, cut the tuna against the grain into tidy 2-cm/1-inch cubes. Marinate in the bowl for 15 minutes.

Chips

Heat up your deep fat fryer, or a large, deep pan half-filled with oil over medium heat. Heat the oil to 140°C/285°F or until a cube of bread dropped in sizzles and browns in 1 minute.

Deep fry the chips for 3 minutes. Remove from the oil with a slotted spoon and set on a board. Stab them several times with a fork to create crispy bits. Return them to the oil and fry again for 2 minutes or until golden. Remove and drain on a kitchen paper/paper towel. Season with salt.

Wasabi mayo

Combine the mayonnaise and wasabi paste.

Scatter the spring onions/scallions over the marinated tuna and serve with the chips and wasabi mayo.

Deep-fried frogs' legs
ếch chiên nước mắm

Frogs' legs

up to 2 litres/8 cups
 sunflower or vegetable
 oil
400 g/14 oz. frogs' legs or
 chicken wings
100 g/¾ cup plain/
 all-purpose flour or
 tapioca starch
1 teaspoon chilli powder
½ teaspoon ground ginger
1 teaspoon cayenne pepper
1 teaspoon sugar
2 teaspoons pork bouillon
1 teaspoon sea salt
200 ml/¾ cup buttermilk or
 double/heavy cream

Sweet chilli dipping sauce

2 Bird's Eye chillies, finely
 chopped
2 garlic cloves, finely
 chopped
2 tablespoons cider vinegar
3 tablespoons sugar
3 tablespoons fish sauce

Garnishes

sliced spring onions/
 scallions
sliced Bird's Eye chillies

deep fat fryer (optional)

Serves 2–4

The Vietnamese love frogs' legs.
This recipe is based on my love
of fried chicken wings, which
are similar to frogs' legs.
I found inspiration for this
during my travels to the
American Deep South.

Frogs' legs

Start to heat up your deep fat fryer, or a large, deep pan
half-filled with oil over medium heat. Heat the oil to
140°C/285°F or until a cube of bread dropped in sizzles
and browns in 1 minute.

Combine the flour, chilli powder, ginger, cayenne,
sugar, bouillon and salt in a bowl. Dip the frogs' legs in
the buttermilk, then in the dry ingredients until coated.

Deep fry the frogs' legs in batches for 4 minutes or
until golden and the juices run clear when you prick the
meat with a knife.

Sweet chilli dipping sauce

Mix all the ingredients in a bowl.

Garnishes

Serve the frogs' legs hot with the garnishes to scatter over
the top and the sweet chilli dipping sauce on the side.

At gatherings, people love to make fresh rolls at the table while they chatter and natter. This recipe doesn't require any cooking as such – the fish is "cooked" by its acidic marinade – so it's lovely for alfresco dinner parties.

Fresh rolls with mackerel ceviche
gỏi cuốn cá thu sống đậu phộng ớt

Fish
1 lemongrass stalk, finely chopped
freshly squeezed juice of 1½ limes and grated zest of 1 lime
4 tablespoons orange juice
2 teaspoons sugar
½ shallot, finely chopped
½ Bird's Eye chilli
2 teaspoons fish sauce
2 large mackerel fillets (about 200 g/7 oz.)

Garnishes
beansprouts
sawtooth, finely chopped (optional) or Thai sweet basil
garden mint
crushed roasted salted peanuts
sliced Bird's Eye chillies, deseeded

Dipping sauce
¼ pineapple, peeled
2 tablespoons fish sauce
2 Bird's Eye chillies
2 garlic cloves
2 tablespoons cider vinegar
2 tablespoons sugar

Filling
100 g/3½ oz. thin rice vermicelli
4–6 rice paper sheets, about 16 cm/6 inches
shiso/perilla leaves (optional)
cockscomb mint (optional)
garden mint
coriander/cilantro

Makes 4–6

Fish
Combine all the ingredients, except the mackerel, in a bowl. With a sharp knife, cut the mackerel on the diagonal, against the grain, into thin slices. Marinate in the bowl for 10–15 minutes, turning the slices gently halfway through.

Garnishes
Blanch the beansprouts in a saucepan of boiling water for 1 minute.

When the fish is ready (it should be "cooked" on the outside and raw on the inside). Sprinkle with the sawtooth, mint, peanuts and chillies.

Dipping sauce
Blitz all the ingredients together in a blender.

Filling
Put the rice vermicelli, a pinch of salt and a dash of vinegar in a bowl or pan of boiling water, cover and allow to cook for 5–10 minutes or until soft. Drain and rinse with hot water.

Pour some warm water into a tray deep and large enough to submerge the rice paper sheets.

Dip a rice paper sheet in the water, put on a plate, fill with the fish, beansprouts and remaining filling ingredients and serve with the dipping sauce.

Bánh xèo is a street-food favourite of many Vietnamese when the sun sets – it is a light savoury crêpe made with rice flour and coconut milk, to be eaten as it's being cooked. It is served with an abundance of salad leaves and herbs. A slice of crêpe is placed on a lettuce leaf in the palm of your hand, then rolled up with lots of herbs and dipped into a fish sauce-based dipping sauce. Never before have I enjoyed a salad so immensely. Everything should be prepped in advance so the crepes can be eaten as soon as they are done.

Sizzling crepes with pork and prawns
bánh xèo thịt heo tôm

Dipping sauce
2 garlic cloves, finely
   chopped
2 Bird's Eye chillies, finely
   chopped
2 tablespoons cider
   vinegar
5 tablespoons fish sauce
3 tablespoons sugar

Crêpes
200 g/1½ cups rice flour
2 teaspoons ground
   turmeric
400 ml/1½ cups coconut
   milk
2 spring onions/scallions,
   thinly sliced
a pinch of sea salt
a pinch of sugar
cooking oil, for frying
4 shallots, chopped
200 g/7 oz. pork belly,
   thinly sliced

400 g/14 oz. king prawns/
   jumbo shrimp, shelled
   and deveined
200 g/3½ cups
   beansprouts
sea salt and black pepper

Garnishes
lettuce leaves
spring onions/scallions,
   cut into short lengths
coriander/cilantro
Thai sweet basil
garden or hot mint

*20-cm/8-inch non-stick
   frying pan with a lid*

Makes about 12

Dipping sauce
Mix together the garlic, chillies and vinegar in a bowl. Set aside for 2 minutes. This "cooks" the garlic. Now add the fish sauce, sugar and 400 ml/1½ cups water.

Crêpes
Mix together the flour, turmeric, coconut milk, 400 ml/1½ cups water, spring onions/scallions, salt and sugar in a bowl, making sure it is smooth and free of lumps.

Heat 1 teaspoon oil in the frying pan over medium heat and fry 1 teaspoon of the chopped shallots until browned. Season the pork belly and prawns/shrimp with salt and pepper and add a few pieces to the pan until cooked through. Using a shallow ladle, pour in a thin layer of the crêpe batter, add a handful of beansprouts and cover the pan with the lid. Allow to cook for 2 minutes. Remove the lid and cook for a further minute, making sure the crêpe is crispy and brown. Fold the crêpe in half and set aside. Repeat this whole process with the remaining shallots, batter and other ingredients to make several more crêpes.

Garnishes
To eat, break a piece of crêpe onto a lettuce leaf, add the onions/scallions and herbs, roll it all up and dip it in the dipping sauce.

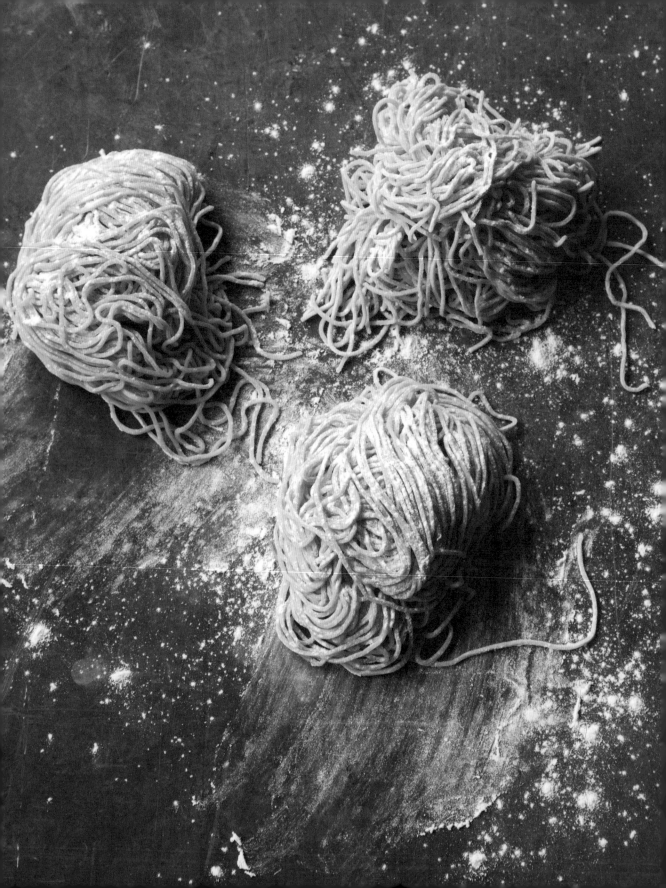

Live Long
Noodles

All of Sài Gòn is perfumed with smoke from honey-grilled pork at lunchtime, and *bún thịt nướng* (grilled/broiled meat on noodles) is a favourite. It is a great example of Vietnamese cuisine: juicy, sweet, savoury and succulent meat with vermicelli, sharp pickles and herbs create layers of flavours and textures.

BBQ pork-belly skewers
bún thịt nướng

400 g/14 oz. pork belly, cut into bite-size pieces
1 lemongrass stalk, finely chopped
1 thumb's worth of galangal, finely chopped (optional)
2 shallots, finely chopped
4 garlic cloves, chopped
1 tablespoon honey
2 teaspoons fish sauce
2 tablespoons cooking oil
1 tablespoon tapioca starch
½ teaspoon black pepper
1 tablespoon sugar
1 teaspoon shrimp paste

Dipping sauce
4 tablespoons cider vinegar
4 tablespoons sugar
4 tablespoons fish sauce
2 garlic cloves, finely chopped
2 Bird's Eye chillies, finely chopped

Noodle salad
300 g/10½ oz. thin rice vermicelli
8 coriander/cilantro stalks, torn
12 Thai sweet basil leaves, torn
12 cockscomb mint leaves (optional)
12 shiso/perilla leaves (optional)
8 lettuce leaves, torn
½ cucumber, julienned
Pickle (page 20)
storebought pickled leeks (optional)
4 tablespoons roasted salted peanuts, crushed

10–12 bamboo skewers

Serves 4

Put the pork, lemongrass, galangal, shallots, garlic, honey, fish sauce, oil, tapioca starch, pepper, sugar and shrimp paste in a bowl. Mix well and rub the mixture into the pork pieces. Marinate in the fridge for 20 minutes. Meanwhile, soak the skewers in water to stop them burning in the oven later.

Preheat the oven to 180°C (350°F) Gas 4, or preheat the grill/broiler.

Push about 3 pork pieces onto each soaked skewer. Cook in the preheated oven for about 18 minutes, or under the preheated grill/broiler for 12–15 minutes, or until well browned.

Dipping sauce
Mix all the ingredients in a bowl with 4 tablespoons hot water.

Noodle salad
Put the rice vermicelli, a pinch of salt and a dash of vinegar in a bowl or pan of boiling water, cover and allow to cook for 5–10 minutes or until soft. Drain and rinse with hot water.

Mix together the herbs, lettuce and cucumber and divide between 4 bowls. Add the noodles, pickle and pickled leeks, if using, on top. Scatter the peanuts over everything. Serve with the pork skewers and dipping sauce.

The French influence

The French left a colossal gastronomic mark during and after their colonization of Vietnam in the late nineteenth century when they created French Indochina.

The famous French baguette and other foods like carrot, tomatoes, potatoes, peas, onions, asparagus, cream, butter, coffee, pâté, milk, custard, cake, flan, croissants, yogurt, omelette, beef and wine were introduced by the French and the love affair began. The Vietnamese re-shaped and re-energized their own cuisine by fusing it with the rich flavours of French food. What is known today of Vietnamese food is that it is intensely delicious and vivid, never failing to capture the hearts of those who taste it.

As French became more widely spoken in Vietnam, French words for ingredients entered the language and remain today. For example, it is believed that *phở* stems from the French word *feu*, meaning "fire", and derives from the French beef casserole *pot au feu* ("pot of fire") containing French ingredients such as beef and charred onion.

The French also introduced beef to the Vietnamese diet, which previously consisted of fish, vegetables and noodles.

Today, floods of people pour out onto the street from coffee houses, and *cà phê* (*café*, ie coffee) is celebrated and drunk en masse with condensed milk (as fresh milk is harder to come by) and ice. Through cafés and coffee culture, people have adopted a French way of life, seeking solace and quiet away from the crowds.

Other nods to France include the love of pastries and cakes – bought from street vendors and air-conditioned boutiques for birthdays and celebrations. And it is common for people to enjoy a *crème caramel* with crushed ice and a glass of coffee in the evening.

These are lovely snacks or starters/appetizers to eat while drinking beer and hanging out with friends. They can be made into a more substantial meal by serving them with a noodle salad or turning them into fresh rolls. The *lá lốt* leaves do not have much fragrance until heated, when they have their own special smell and taste – similar to cinnamon, sesame and pepper. The steak can be used in a stir-fry without the leaves and served with rice noodles.

Lemongrass beef in betel leaves
bò lá lốt

300 g/10½ oz. rump/ round steak, very thinly sliced
1 lemongrass stalk, finely chopped
3 garlic cloves, finely chopped
1 teaspoon dried chilli flakes/dried hot pepper flakes
1 tablespoon sugar
½ teaspoon sea salt
2½ tablespoons sesame oil
1 tablespoon sesame seeds
1 tablespoon cooking oil
1 tablespoon honey
¼ kiwi, finely chopped
150 g/5½ oz. betel leaves (or shiso/perilla), stalks removed, then washed and dried

Dipping sauce
2 Bird's Eye chillies, deseeded and finely chopped
1 garlic clove, finely chopped
1½ tablespoons sugar
2 tablespoons cider vinegar
2 tablespoons fish sauce
3 tablespoons roasted salted peanuts, crushed

Noodle salad
300 g/10½ oz. thin rice vermicelli
lettuce leaves
Thai sweet basil
coriander/cilantro
cockscomb mint
shiso/perilla
Pickle (page 20)

Serves 4–6

Put the steak, lemongrass, garlic, dried chilli flakes/ hot pepper flakes, sugar, salt, 1 teaspoon of the sesame oil, the sesame seeds, cooking oil, honey and kiwi in a bowl. Mix well and rub the mixture into the steak slices. Marinate in the fridge for 20 minutes.

Preheat the oven to 180°C (350°F) Gas 4.

Place a betel leaf in front of you, shiny side up and spine pointing straight ahead and away from you. Put a couple of slices of the steak across the leaf, then roll it up as tightly as you can. The roll should be the thickness of your index finger. Place it, seam side down, in a roasting pan. Repeat this process until all the leaves and filling have been used up and arrange the rolls snugly next to each other in the pan to prevent them from unrolling. Drizzle the remaining sesame oil over the rolls and bake in the preheated oven for 12 minutes for medium–rare.

Dipping sauce
Mix all the ingredients in a bowl.

Noodle salad
Put the rice vermicelli, a pinch of salt and a dash of vinegar in a bowl or pan of boiling water, cover and allow to cook for 5–10 minutes or until soft. Drain and rinse with hot water.

Divide the noodles between 4–6 bowls and serve with the rolls, lettuce, herbs and pickle, and dipping sauce for dipping or drizzling over the rolls.

Phở noodles (also known as "ho fun" and used in *phở* soup) are fabulous for dry stir-fry dishes, as they are quick and easy to cook. You can use any vegetables you like in this dish and make it as simple or colourful as you wish. Prepare everything before starting so that nothing gets overcooked.

Stir-fried beef and fresh noodles
phở xào bò

2 tablespoons cooking oil
200 g/7 oz. sirloin or
 rump/round steak,
 thinly sliced
120 g/1⅓ cups sugarsnap
 peas (or mangetout/
 snow peas, sliced
 courgettes/zucchini
 or leafy greens)
3 tablespoons oyster
 sauce
4 tablespoons soy sauce
splash of white wine or
 water
a pinch of black pepper
1 garlic clove, sliced
½ onion, chopped
400 g/14 oz. fresh *phở* (ho
 fun) noodles, separated
 (if using dry, cook
 according to package
 instructions)
80 g/1½ cups
 beansprouts (optional)

Dipping sauce (optional)
3 tablespoons soy sauce
1 Bird's Eye chilli, sliced

Serves 2

Heat a dash of oil in a frying pan or wok over high heat until very hot, then fry the steak, sugarsnaps, 1 tablespoon of the oyster sauce, 2 tablespoons of the soy sauce, a dash of the wine, the pepper and garlic for a couple of minutes or until the steak is cooked as you like it. Transfer the contents of the pan to a plate and allow to rest.

Heat another dash of oil in the pan again, then stir-fry the onion for a few seconds. Add the noodles and the remaining oyster and soy sauces. Stir-fry for a couple of minutes. Add the beansprouts and a dash more wine. Stir-fry for a further minute.

Dipping sauce (optional)
Crush the chilli into the soy sauce with the back of a spoon.

Serve the rested beef mixture and stir-fried noodles with the dipping sauce.

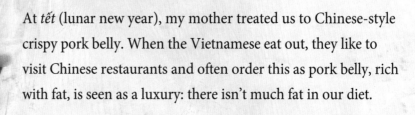

At *tết* (lunar new year), my mother treated us to Chinese-style crispy pork belly. When the Vietnamese eat out, they like to visit Chinese restaurants and often order this as pork belly, rich with fat, is seen as a luxury: there isn't much fat in our diet.

Crispy marinated pork belly
bánh hỏi thịt quay

1 tablespoon bicarbonate of/baking soda
1 kg/2 lbs. 3 oz. pork belly
1 tablespoon soy sauce
1 teaspoon Chinese five-spice powder
½ teaspoon pork bouillon
1½ teaspoons sea salt
freshly squeezed juice of 1 lime

Noodles
300 g/10½ oz. thin rice vermicelli
1 tablespoon cooking oil
2 spring onions/scallions, finely chopped

Dipping sauce
2 garlic cloves, finely chopped
2 Bird's Eye chillies, finely chopped
2 tablespoons cider vinegar
5 tablespoons fish sauce
3 tablespoons sugar

Garnishes
coriander/cilantro
Thai sweet basil
garden or hot mint
storebought pickled leeks

Serves 4

Bring a large saucepan of water to the boil, add the bicarbonate of/baking soda and pork belly and poach it over medium heat for about 5 minutes. Drain, then scrape any scum off the pork skin with a knife and pat dry. Now stab the pork all over with the knife and pat dry again.

Combine the soy sauce, five-spice, bouillon and ½ teaspoon of the salt, then rub it over the meat side of the pork. Pat dry to absorb any excess liquid. Rub ½ teaspoon of the salt and half the lime juice over the skin side of the pork. Pat dry to absorb any excess liquid. If possible, hang the meat up (over a plate) to allow it to dry out nicely. Allow it to marinate at room temperature for about 30 minutes.

Preheat the oven to 200°C (400°F) Gas 6.

Rub the remaining salt and lime juice into the pork skin. Pat dry again. Place, meat side up, on a baking sheet and roast in the preheated oven for 30 minutes.

Raise the temperature to 220°C (425°F) Gas 7, turn the pork over and roast, skin side up, for 1 hour or until the skin is crispy and crackly. Allow the pork to cool slightly, then cut into bite-size pieces.

Noodles
Put the rice vermicelli, a pinch of salt and a dash of vinegar in a pan of boiling water, cover with a lid and cook for 3–5 minutes until soft. Drain and rinse with hot water.

Heat the oil in a frying pan over medium heat and fry the spring onions/scallions for 1 minute. Toss with the noodles.

Dipping sauce
Mix together the garlic, chillies and vinegar in a bowl. Set aside for 2 minutes. This "cooks" the garlic. Now add the fish sauce, sugar and 400 ml/1½ cups water.

Garnishes
Serve the crispy pork belly at room temperature with garnishes, dipping sauce and noodles.

My mother excels at making the best of what she has, especially in her kitchen cupboard. This is particularly true of peanuts, which she adds to lots of dishes to add texture and make every bite crunchy and rich. Here, they contrast with the very silky glass (cellophane) noodles, and each and every simple and modest ingredient stands out.

Stir-fried noodles and beansprouts
miến xào giá đậu phộng lá hẹ

200 g/7 oz. glass
   (cellophane) noodles
dash of cooking oil
2 Asian shallots, finely
   chopped
3 tablespoons light soy
   sauce
a pinch of black pepper
a pinch of pork or vegetable
   bouillon (optional)
1 Bird's Eye chilli, thinly
   sliced
100 ml/⅓ cup white wine
   or water

160 g/2¾ cups beansprouts
handful of garlic chives, cut
   into 2-cm/1-inch lengths
   (optional), or garden mint
2 sprigs of coriander/
   cilantro, chopped
2 big tablespoons roasted
   salted peanuts, crushed

Dipping sauce (optional)
3 tablespoons soy sauce
1 Bird's Eye chilli, sliced

Serves 2

Put the noodles in a bowl, cover with warm water and allow to soak for 30 minutes. After 30 minutes, cut them into shorter lengths.

Heat the oil in a frying pan over low–medium heat and fry the shallots for about 5 minutes. Add the noodles, soy sauce, pepper and bouillon, if using, and stir-fry for 2–3 minutes.

Add the chilli, wine and beansprouts. Stir-fry for 2 minutes, then remove from the heat and mix in the garlic chives, coriander/cilantro and peanuts. Serve hot or at room temperature.

Dipping sauce (optional)
Crush the chilli into the soy sauce with the back of a spoon.

This recipe has a Chinese flavour, as the leaves are widely used in Cantonese cuisine. The simplicity of the dish is what makes it so appetizing, with sweet shallots, sesame-tossed noodles and a slightly bitter broccoli flavour.

Egg noodles with Chinese broccoli
mì xào rau cải ngọt

150 g/5 oz. fresh egg
  noodles
2 tablespoons light soy
  sauce
1 teaspoon cider vinegar
1 tablespoon sugar
2 tablespoons cooking oil
2 Asian shallots, finely diced
splash of sesame oil

4 sprigs of Chinese broccoli/
  kai-lan (or bok choy, choi
  sum, spinach, watercress,
  kale, sprout tops,
  asparagus)
chilli oil with shrimp
  (optional), or Sriracha
  chilli sauce

Serves 2

Put the noodles in a saucepan of boiling water and blanch for 1 minute. Drain, rinse with hot water and allow to drain well in a colander.

Mix together the soy sauce, vinegar and sugar.

Heat the cooking oil in a large saucepan and fry the shallots until golden brown. Stir in the soy mixture, then remove from the heat.

Put the noodles on a serving dish, tip the shallots and soy mixture over the top, add a dash of sesame oil and toss together.

Put the broccoli/kai-lan in a bowl, cover with boiling water and blanch for 1 minute. Drain, then season with a dash of sesame oil and place on top of the noodles. Season with chilli oil or chilli sauce.

Bánh cuốn are noodle sheets similar to lasagne, traditionally made from rice flour, tapioca starch and water and then steamed. They are folded or rolled, with or without a filling, and dipped into a *nước chấm*. As they are light yet full of carbohydrates, they are eaten for breakfast or lunch. My aunt makes them every morning outside her home in Vietnam and steams them over a charcoal fire but my mother came up with the idea of cooking the batter like a pancake.

Rice rolls with pork and prawns
bánh cuốn nhân thịt tôm nấm meo

Filling
80 g/1 cup dried shredded wood ear mushrooms
dash of cooking oil
2 Asian shallots, finely chopped
300 g/10½ oz. minced/ground chicken or pork
½ teaspoon sea salt
½ teaspoon coarsely ground black pepper
2 teaspoons sugar
170 g/6 oz. king prawns/jumbo shrimp, shelled, deveined and finely chopped

Noodle sheets
300 g/2¼ cups tapioca starch
300 g/2¼ cups rice flour
1 teaspoon cooking oil, plus extra for frying
2 spring onions/scallions, finely chopped
½ teaspoon salt

Dressing
2 garlic cloves, finely chopped
2 Bird's Eye chillies, finely chopped
2 tablespoons cider vinegar
5 tablespoons fish sauce
3 tablespoons sugar

Garnishes
deep-fried shallots
Thai sweet basil, finely chopped
coriander/cilantro, finely chopped

20-cm/8-inch non-stick frying pan with a lid

Serves 6

Filling
Put the mushrooms in a bowl, cover with warm water and soak for at least 30 minutes. Drain and pat dry.

Heat the oil in a frying pan and fry the shallots briefly. Add the meat and mushrooms and stir-fry for a couple of minutes. Add the salt, pepper, sugar and prawns/shrimp. Cook for 3 minutes, then allow to rest.

Noodle sheets
Mix the ingredients and 900 ml/scant 4 cups water in a bowl, making sure it is smooth and free of lumps. Heat a dash of oil in the 20-cm/8-inch frying pan. Using a shallow ladle, pour in 1 ladleful of the batter and tilt the pan to spread the batter. Cover with the lid and cook for 2 minutes, then slide the cooked noodle sheet onto a plate. Repeat with the remaining batter.

Divide the filling between the noodle sheets. Fold the sides over the filling, then roll up tightly from the bottom. Place, seam side down, on a serving dish.

Dressing
Mix together the garlic, chillies and vinegar in a bowl. Set aside for 2 minutes. This "cooks" the garlic. Now add the fish sauce, sugar and 400 ml/1½ cups water.

Garnishes
Serve the rolls warm or at room temperature with the garnishes and dressing sprinkled on top.

Stir-fried udon noodles and vegetables
bánh canh xào chay

In Vietnamese cooking, the work is in the preparation, with very little time on the stove. My friends are always amazed that I can pull together a fried noodle dish when I haven't slaved all day in the kitchen. This recipe is a great way of using vegetables for a light meal. Adapt it with any kind of noodles and vegetables you have. You can add herbs like coriander/cilantro, garden mint or Thai sweet basil for something nutritious.

2 tablespoons cooking oil
½ red onion, sliced
400 g/14 oz. fresh udon noodles
a pinch of sugar
a pinch of sea salt
a pinch of black pepper
1 teaspoon light soy sauce
250 ml/1 cup white wine or water
2 Asian shallots or ½ red onion, diced
1 carrot, cut into matchsticks
4 stems of purple sprouting broccoli, roughly chopped
a small handful of mangetout/snow peas
1 tablespoon oyster sauce
40 g/½ cup beansprouts
1 head of bok choy, roughly chopped
1 tablespoon crushed roasted salted peanuts or cashew nuts

Serves 2

Heat the oil in a frying pan or wok and fry the onion until softened. Add the noodles, sugar, salt, pepper, and soy sauce and fry, stirring quickly (with cooking chopsticks if you have them) for 5 minutes. Add a splash of wine to steam the noodles, and keep separating them so that they don't stick together.

Transfer the mixture to a plate. In the same hot pan or wok, heat another dash of oil, then fry the shallots until browned. Add the carrot, broccoli, mangetout/snow peas and oyster sauce and stir-fry for 3 minutes. Now add the beansprouts and a cupful of wine to help steam the vegetables and cook for 2 minutes. Add the bok choy at the last minute.

Remove the pan from the heat, add the noodle mixture and stir well. Sprinkle with nuts and serve hot or at room temperature.

Eat and Play
Lunch and Dinner

Table etiquette

If you are the youngest member of the family, you will have a lot of salutations to do when you sit down to eat. You begin by addressing the eldest member of the family and work your way down. No one ever greets anyone younger than themselves; everyone is ranked by age in honour and respect. You might say "*moi* grandfather", "*moi* grandmother" etc, meaning *bon appétit* and inviting the person to enjoy the food.

There is a place for everybody at the table or on the floor; the cook brings to the table the rice pot, fish and/or meat dishes, vegetable stir-fries and a palate-cleansing soup. Everyone has a bowl for rice, a pair of chopsticks and a spoon for soup. Depending on your religion and how devoted you are, prayers are said to give thanks.

Vietnamese people tend to eat lunch and dinner at home so they can be close to their family. At home, there is usually incense burning to give worship to Buddha, past ancestors and spirits of the land. Sometimes, if a family member has passed away, a place is set for them so that they are not forgotten and they can be well fed in their new reincarnated life.

In a culture where giving is essential to good karma, food eaten around the table is all about sharing. Everybody eats from the dishes in the middle. Each delicious morsel is taken, but then may be offered to someone else. It is polite to put just a small amount in your rice bowl, then return for more. It is never acceptable to take the biggest pieces, leaving others with less. The cook will usually have a naturally hospitable "feeder" mentality and make more than enough to go around. It is always encouraging to ask for more rice, eat lots, polish off your food, burp and compliment the cook by saying "*ngon quá!*"

Raw beef and starfruit salad
gỏi rau muống khế thịt bò tái

Beef
200 g/7 oz. rump/round or sirloin steak, very thinly sliced
1 tablespoon tamarind paste
freshly squeezed juice of 2 limes
2 tablespoons orange juice
½ teaspoon shrimp paste
2 tablespoons mirin

Dressing
2 tablespoons honey
1 Asian shallot, finely chopped
½ lemongrass stalk (outer layer removed), very finely chopped
2 tablespoons fish sauce
1 garlic clove, finely chopped
freshly squeezed juice of ½ lime

Salad
100 g/2 cups curly morning glory
1 starfruit, thinly sliced
1 Bird's Eye chilli, thinly sliced (optional)

Serves 2

"Why don't the stars fall from the sky?" asked my inquisitive four-year-old self, perched on the lap of my young aunt on our Sài Gòn balcony filled with pink bougainvillea and green floral tiles. "Those ones are coming" she replied, pointing to the night sky. "Mind your head when they come, for they will make your heart faint and gooey" and she dipped the sweetest starfruit with salt and chilli into my mouth. She played havoc with my young mind, telling stories of Tintin, the boy who lives on the moon, and the grape tree taking root in my belly. We danced around cherry trees and feasted on mangosteen, custard apples and rambutans. This salad reminds me of her and the crazy imagination she gifted me.

Beef
Combine all the ingredients in a shallow bowl. Marinate for 20 minutes, for medium–rare, or longer if you prefer the beef more "cooked".

Dressing
Mix all the ingredients in a bowl.

Salad
Put the curly morning glory and starfruit on a serving dish. Remove the beef from the marinade (discard the marinade) and add to the salad. Serve with the dressing drizzled over the top.

You can use watercress instead of curly morning glory, if you prefer.

Cơm tấm are broken and fractured rice grains! They are small and easily digestible and pair fantastically with pork chops. In Sài Gòn, in hundreds of lunch diners, the noise is immense as waiters carry out 6 broken-rice dishes on each arm to feed the hungry and eager. The rice is usually eaten with a spoon and the pork chop is stabbed with a fork and brought up to the mouth to tear off delicious chunks.

Pork, egg pudding and broken rice
cơm tấm sườn nướng trứng hấp

1 lemongrass stalk, finely
   chopped
2 Bird's Eye chillies, finely
   chopped
2 garlic cloves, finely
   chopped
1 teaspoon pork bouillon
1 teaspoon sugar
1 teaspoon soy sauce
2 pork chops
200 g/1¼ cups broken rice
1 spring onion/scallion,
   thinly sliced
dash of cooking oil

Egg pudding
3 tablespoons dried
   shredded wood ear
   mushrooms
2 eggs
2 tablespoons minced/
   ground pork
1 Asian shallot, finely
   chopped
a pinch of black pepper
1 teaspoon pork bouillon

Dressing
2 garlic cloves, finely
   chopped
2 Bird's Eye chillies, finely
   chopped
3 tablespoons cider
   vinegar
3 tablespoons sugar
4 tablespoons fish sauce

Garnishes
a selection of herbs of
   your choice, such as
   coriander/cilantro,
   garden mint, Thai
   sweet basil, shiso/
   perilla or cockscomb
   mint
Pickle (page 20)
cucumber slices

steamer
baking sheet, greased

Serves 2

Mix the lemongrass, chillies, garlic, bouillon, sugar and soy sauce in a shallow bowl. Add the pork and marinate in the fridge for at least 20 minutes.

Cook the rice according to the package instructions – about 20 minutes. Fry the spring onion/scallion in the oil for 1 minute and scatter over the rice.

Preheat the oven to 180°C (350°F) Gas 4.

Put the pork on the prepared baking sheet and cook for 12–15 minutes on each side or until golden and the juices run clear when you stick a knife in.

Egg pudding
Put the wood ear mushrooms in a bowl, cover with warm water and allow to soak for at least 30 minutes. When ready, drain the mushrooms and pat them dry.

Mix all the ingredients well, pour into a porcelain or metal bowl and steam in a steamer for 15 minutes.

Dressing
Mix all the ingredients in a bowl.

Garnishes
Serve the chops, rice and a slice of egg pudding with herbs, pickle, cucumber and the dressing.

The French baking powder, Alsa Levure Chimique "Alsacienne", is an ingredient widely used in Vietnamese cuisine, especially in fishcakes. It acts as a raising agent and holds the fish together without having to use another ingredient like potatoes, so what you are eating is just fish. For a starter/appetizer, these can be wrapped in Chinese mustard greens and dipped in chilli sauce; or they can be sliced and eaten in baguettes, with rice and fish sauce, stir-fries and noodle soups.

Fishcakes with dill
cá thác lác thìa là

300 g/10½ oz. skinless haddock or monkfish fillets, chopped

1 Asian shallot, chopped

1 Bird's Eye chilli

1½ teaspoons sugar

1 teaspoon French baking powder (Alsa Levure Chimique "Alsacienne")

a pinch of black pepper

2 tablespoons cooking oil, plus extra for oiling and frying

2 tablespoons fish sauce

1 tablespoon tapioca starch

a handful of dill

steamer (optional)

Serves 4 as a starter/ appetizer

Put all the ingredients in a food processor and process until fine and well combined. Transfer the mixture to a bowl, cover and allow to rest for 1–2 hours or overnight – in which case, put it in the refrigerator.

Rub a little oil onto your hands. Pull small pieces off the rested mixture and roll into balls between your hands. Alternatively, shape the mixture into 1 large or 2 smaller patties.

Steam the balls or fishcakes for 5 minutes in a steamer. They can then be refrigerated or frozen, to be fried at a later date. You can also poach them in broth for noodle soups (see page 42).

To serve, heat a dash of oil in a frying pan and fry the balls or fishcakes, stirring or turning a couple of times, until golden brown all over. Leave the balls whole, but slice the fishcakes.

Any white fish, salmon or trout can be used in place of the haddock or monkfish.

This very plain and uncomplex recipe is deceptive in its modesty because it is really tasty! Fasting on Buddha's vegetarian diet could be so very enjoyable. Vegetarianism is not required in order to follow Buddha's path, however, on fasting days, strict Buddhists follow a vegetarian diet to adhere to the principles of non-violence and are prohibited from harming plant (root vegetables) or animal life. As this recipe contains fish sauce, it wouldn't be suitable for a strict fast, but is fine for a semi-strict one. Herbs, fruits and vegetables grow in abundance in Vietnam, so side dishes such as this can accompany fish and meat dishes.

Tofu and tomatoes in fish sauce
đậu phụ sốt cà chua

250 g/9 oz. fresh tofu, cut into 9 cubes
2½ tablespoons cooking oil
1 garlic clove, finely chopped
1 Asian shallot, finely chopped
3 tomatoes, quartered
2 spring onions/scallions, chopped
2 tablespoons mirin
1 tablespoon fish sauce
cooked rice or rice vermicelli, to serve (optional)

Serves 2–3

Pat the tofu fry.

Heat 2 tablespoons of the oil in a frying pan over medium heat and fry the tofu until golden all over – about 7 minutes. Remove from the heat and place on kitchen paper/paper towels to soak up the excess oil.

Heat the remaining oil in the frying pan and fry the garlic and shallots until softened, then add the tomatoes and spring onions/scallions. Don't stir the tomatoes for a couple of minutes to encourage them to brown on one side, then gently turn them over. Fry for about 4 minutes.

Add the tofu, the mirin and fish sauce and fry for 2–3 minutes, stirring gently.

Serve with cooked rice or rice vermicelli. Garnish with garden or hot mint, Thai sweet basil or coriander/cilantro, if you like.

Homemade ham
chả chiên

500 g/1 lb. minced/
  ground pork (shoulder)
  or chicken
½ tablespoon (½ sachet)
  French baking powder
  (Alsa Levure Chimique
  "Alsacienne")
1 tablespoon sugar

2 tablespoons cooking oil,
  plus extra for oiling and
  frying
2 tablespoons fish sauce

steamer

**Serves 4 as a starter/
appetizer**

Like the Fishcakes with Dill on page
100, this recipe also uses French
baking powder. *Chả* is a staple in
Vietnamese cuisine and can be
found in every household, wrapped
in banana leaves. It is normally
consumed with *bánh mì*, noodle
soups and rice dishes. There are many
variations depending on the region,
for example other spices can be added
to the ground/minced meat. When
returning from a trip, it is typical to
bring home that region's *chả* as a gift.

Put all the ingredients and 2 tablespoons water
in a food processor and process until fine and well
combined. Transfer the mixture to a bowl, cover
and refrigerate for about 4 hours or overnight.

Rub a little oil onto your hands. Shape the rested
mixture into a large patty.

Grease the surface of the steamer and steam the
ham for 5 minutes, or until the juices run clear when
you stick a knife in.

When ready to serve, heat a dash of oil in a frying
pan and fry the patty, turning a couple of times, until
golden brown all over.

Fried tilapia with green mango
cá rô phi chiên xoài xanh

1 tablespoon vegetable oil
1 whole red tilapia (or lemon sole, dab, brill, black tilapia, red snapper or pomfret), scaled and gutted
¼ unripened green mango, julienned
cooked rice, to serve

Dressing
2 tablespoons cider vinegar
2 tablespoons sugar
2 tablespoons fish sauce
2 garlic cloves, finely chopped
2 Bird's Eye chillies, finely chopped

Serves 2

The traditional Vietnamese diet is healthy. Meals revolve around rice, vegetables and fish. The fish here has a crunchy, crispy skin and soft flesh, complemented by crunchy and sour unripe mango. The mango must be green and unripe as the sour flavour balances perfectly with the sweet *nước chấm* dressing. This is a meal that leaves you wanting more and more.

Heat the oil in a large frying pan over low–medium heat, then put the whole tilapia in the pan. Fry for 10 minutes on each side, or until golden, crispy and cooked through.

Dressing
Mix all the ingredients in a bowl.

Lay out the mango on a serving dish. Place the tilapia on top and drizzle with the dressing.

Serve with cooked rice.

Pan-fried grey mullet with tomatoes
cá chiên sốt cà chua

As fish and rice are eaten almost every day, there are always attempts to jazz them up for variety. One traditional way is with a tomato sauce. It is no wonder the Vietnamese love Italian food so much – they have a passionate love affair with tomatoes! This sauce is excellent with kingfish or mackerel, as well as grey mullet.

3 tablespoons cooking oil
500-g/1-lb. whole grey mullet (or kingfish, mackerel, sea bass, seabream, salmon, trout or carp), skin on, gutted and cut into thick steaks
sea salt
1 tablespoon cornflour/cornstarch
½ teaspoon pork bouillon
a pinch of black pepper

½ teaspoon sugar
2 garlic cloves, finely chopped
1 Asian shallot, finely chopped
2 tomatoes, cut into wedges
1 spring onion/scallion, chopped
coriander/cilantro
cooked rice, to serve

Serves 2

Heat half the oil in a frying over medium heat, then add the fish steaks and season with a little salt. Fry them for 3 minutes on each side, then transfer to a dish and set aside.

In a small bowl, mix together 5 tablespoons water, the cornflour/cornstarch, bouillon, pepper and sugar.

Heat the remaining oil in the frying pan and fry the garlic, shallot and tomatoes for about 3 minutes. Add the cornflour/cornstarch mixture to the pan and stir well for a couple of minutes until slightly thickened. Transfer to a serving dish.

Place the fish steaks in the dish and top with the spring onion/scallion and coriander/cilantro. Serve with cooked rice.

Inspired by a Hong-Kong style steamed fish recipe, this is one of the easiest and tastiest things to make and eat. It can be enjoyed with steamed rice or put in the centre of the table to dig into alongside rice paper and vermicelli. It was one of the first things I made when I started cooking as a twenty-something, fresh out of home and missing my mum. She worked long hours to make a living, so although she was keen to cook, she didn't always have much time – this took just minutes to prepare but tasted amazing.

Baked seabream
cá nướng xì dầu hành lá

1 tablespoon cooking oil
2 x 300–500-g/11–18-oz. whole seabream (or carp, sea bass or trout), scaled and gutted
1 thumb's worth of fresh ginger, peeled and julienned
1 lemon, sliced and skin cut off
2 red onions, quartered
1 tablespoon vegetable oil
cooked rice and fried greens, to serve

Dressing
1 tablespoon cooking oil
2 spring onion/scallions, 1 finely chopped and 1 shredded
6 tablespoons soy sauce
1 tablespoon cider vinegar
1 tablespoon sugar
1 tablespoon Sriracha chilli sauce

Serves 4

Preheat the oven to 180°C (350°F) Gas 4.

Drizzle the cooking oil on a baking sheet, place the fish on it and stuff the gut with ginger. Place the lemon slices on top of the fish and scatter the onion quarters around it. Drizzle with the vegetable oil and bake in the preheated oven for 45 minutes.

Dressing

Heat the oil in a saucepan over medium heat, then fry the finely chopped spring onions/scallions for 1 minute. Add the soy sauce, vinegar, sugar and chilli sauce, mix well and bring to a gentle boil.

Once the fish is baked, pour the dressing over it and serve with the fresh, shredded spring onions/scallions. Serve with cooked rice and fried greens.

Water spinach, or water morning glory, was once a staple vegetable of the poor, easily grown in water in canals and next to rice paddies. It is delicious and versatile and works well with simple ingredients like garlic, oyster sauce or shrimp paste. It is eaten all the time with fish and meat dishes at lunch or dinner. Every part of the vegetable should be eaten, especially the crunchy, hollow stalks. Like spinach, it wilts easily and should be flash-fried to maintain its bite.

Stir-fried water spinach
rau muống xào tỏi

dash of cooking oil
½ teaspoon shrimp paste
   (optional)
200 g/7 oz. water spinach/
   water morning glory,
   cut into 10-cm/
   4-inch pieces, stalks on
2 tablespoons oyster
   sauce
2 garlic cloves, finely
   chopped

Serves 2–4

Heat the oil in a frying pan or wok over high heat. When it's very hot, add the shrimp paste, if using, the water spinach, oyster sauce and garlic and stir-fry for about 2 minutes or until the leaves wilt.

   Serve immediately.

   Alternatively, you can use watercress, spinach, bok choy, Chinese cabbage or choi sum in place of the water spinach, if you prefer.

This dish brings me so much pleasure! It's a recipe I learned from my cousins Thúy and Thảo in Vietnam. It makes me so happy to eat this with steamed rice, as all the flavours combine together like a ray of sunshine. As with most dinner recipes, all the work here is in the preparation and it only needs flash cooking on the stove. Sweet and sour recipes like this encompass Vietnamese cuisine in flavour, texture and balance, as well as embodying the character of Vietnamese people in all their glory.

Sweet and sour squid stir-fry
mực xào chua ngọt

250 g/9 oz. squid with tentacles, cleaned
1 garlic clove
2 teaspoons sugar
1 Bird's Eye chilli, half deseeded
3 tablespoons fish sauce
dash of cooking oil
½ onion, cut into bite-size pieces
1 celery stalk, thickly sliced (reserve the leaves for later)
3 tomatoes, cut into wedges

½ courgette/zucchini, cut into bite-size pieces
10 cm/4 inches cucumber, cut into bite-size pieces
200 g/7 oz. fresh or canned pineapple
100 ml/⅓ cup pineapple juice or orange juice
freshly squeezed juice of 1 lime or lemon
cooked rice, to serve
coriander/cilantro and garden mint (optional)

Serves 2–3

Cut the squid into 7-mm/¼-inch rings and keep the tentacles whole.

Put the garlic, sugar and chilli in a mortar and pestle and crush to a paste, then stir in the fish sauce.

Heat the oil in a frying pan or wok over high heat. When it's very hot, add the onion, celery and tomatoes and stir-fry for 1 minute.

Add the courgette/zucchini, cucumber, pineapple and pineapple juice and stir well. Add the squid and garlic paste. Cook for 2–3 minutes, then add the lime juice and stir well.

Garnish with the celery leaves, coriander/cilantro and mint, if using. Serve immediately with cooked rice.

Caramelized sardines in coconut water
cá mòi kho

1 tablespoon cooking oil

½ red onion, finely chopped

350 g/12 oz. whole sardines, scaled and gutted

150 ml/⅔ cup coconut water (or use fresh water plus 1 teaspoon sugar)

1 Bird's Eye chilli

a pinch of black pepper

1 teaspoon coconut caramel

1 teaspoon sugar

1 tablespoon fish sauce

1 teaspoon vegetable oil

cooked rice, to serve

Serves 2

I have lived in Hackney, London, since I was five years old but my mother brought me and my brother up on a strict Vietnamese diet. We loved school dinners because it was different and exotic compared to what we had at home. However, nobody at school liked school dinners very much and decided to go on strike! My brother and I bowed to peer pressure, joined the strike and told my mum to make us some packed lunches. She made us each a tiffin box with rice, soup and sardines caramelized in fish sauce and coconut water. Today I jump for joy at the prospect of this meal, but then, I was ten years old! My friends hadn't even heard of Vietnam and you can imagine what they thought of the sardine smell coming from our rucksacks!

Heat the cooking oil in a frying pan over medium heat and fry the onion until browned.

Add the sardines to the pan and fry for about 2 minutes on each side.

Add the coconut water, chilli, pepper, coconut caramel, sugar, fish sauce and vegetable oil. Bring to the boil, then cover with a lid and simmer over low heat for 20 minutes.

Serve with cooked rice, or a palate-cleansing soup and fried greens.

NOTES If you cannot find coconut caramel, melt and caramelize some palm sugar or raw cane sugar to colour the dish.

The photograph opposite shows double quantities of this recipe.

I adapted this mouthwatering recipe to include English mustard, an ingredient that makes my carnivorous cousins in Vietnam crazy in love for these spareribs – they polish off every last shred of meat. My cousins are convinced that a Vietnamese person loves sucking on bones and fish heads because that way nothing goes to waste and everything is eaten and appreciated in the belly.

BBQ spareribs
sườn heo nướng

4 Asian shallots, finely chopped
1 large garlic clove, finely chopped
4 teaspoons English mustard
4 teaspoons soy sauce
6 tablespoons hoisin sauce
1 tablespoon Sriracha chilli sauce
1 teaspoon honey
800 g/1¾ lbs. pork spareribs or chicken wings
1 teaspoon sesame seeds (optional)

Serves 4–6

In a bowl, mix together all the ingredients (except the meat) to make a marinade. Add the meat and rub the marinade in well. Cover and refrigerate for at least 30 minutes.

Preheat the oven to 200°C (400°F) Gas 6.

Transfer the meat to a roasting pan and roast in the preheated oven for 45 minutes or until cooked through and the juices run clear when you stick a knife in. The meat can also be grilled on a barbecue, in which case times will vary, so check that it's cooked through before serving.

Scatter the sesame seeds over the top before serving, if using.

This marinade can also be used for chicken thighs and drumsticks and pork chops.

Pork and quail's eggs in pear cider
thịt heo kho trứng

This is one of my favourite meals. It can be savoured throughout the week over some steamed rice, with fried greens and a green, leafy soup. It's also a traditional New Year's offering, a peasant dish using cheap cuts of the pork and eggs from the farm. As this can be left on the stove for a few days (you should heat it up twice daily in hot weather so that it doesn't go off), the more you heat it, the more the meat falls apart so you can stretch out the meat to last. The delicious broth flavours rice beautifully too, which means you can make this your meal for days and days to come – really useful if you are on a budget.

This is a sweet, savoury and hot dish, and a reassuring balm for the soul.

12 quail's eggs and/or 4 hen's eggs
1 tablespoon cooking oil
3 Asian shallots or 1 medium onion, finely chopped
3 garlic cloves, finely chopped
800 g–1 kg/1¾–2 lbs. pork belly (skin removed), cubed
250 ml/1 cup pear cider (or [hard] apple cider)
300 ml/1¼ cups coconut water
2 tablespoons coconut caramel
4 tablespoons fish sauce
a pinch of black pepper
4 Bird's Eye chillies
cooked rice, to serve

Serves 2–4

Put all the eggs in a saucepan, cover with cold water and bring to a simmer. Once simmering, cook the quail's eggs for 5 minutes (then fish them out of the pan) and the hen's eggs for 6½ minutes. Run cold water over all the cooked eggs, then peel and set aside.

Heat the oil in a large saucepan over medium heat and fry the shallots and garlic for about 5 minutes. Add half the meat and fry, stirring, to colour off, then fry the remainder. Add the cider, coconut water and coconut caramel. The meat should be submerged, so add more cider, coconut water or fresh water if not. Bring to a gentle boil. Skim off any scum from the surface with a spoon, then season with the fish sauce and pepper.

Add the eggs and chillies to the pan, cover with a lid and simmer over low heat for at least 2 hours.

Serve with cooked rice; it's also delicious with a fried egg.

NOTE If you cannot find coconut caramel, melt and caramelize some palm sugar or raw cane sugar to colour the dish.

Whenever I return to Sài Gòn, my cousins plead with me to make *mì Ý* – spaghetti bolognese! It's their most favourite dish and Italian eateries are blossoming everywhere in the new cosmopolitan Vietnam where Italian food is adored. They say they crave it so much that their mouths water and they must go and eat it somewhere just to satisfy their taste buds. Even though I have given them instructions on how to make it, they keep saying they can't get it right because they don't know the foreign way of cooking. This Italian recipe is especially for my cousins who appreciate and pine for Italian food. I've added a good-quality fish sauce to enhance the perfect umami flavour.

Spaghetti bolognese
mì Ý

1 tablespoon cooking oil
2 celery stalks, sliced (reserve the leaves for later)
¼ leek, thinly sliced
1 red onion, chopped
2 small carrots, finely chopped
500 g/1 lb. minced/ground beef
2 garlic cloves, chopped
160 ml/⅔ cup extra dry vermouth or fortified wine
3 tablespoons fish sauce
500 g/1 lb. tomatoes, chopped
400 g/14 oz. canned chopped tomatoes
2 bay leaves
150 g/2 cups sliced button (or other small) mushrooms
1 beef stock cube
400 g/14 oz. dried spaghetti

Garnishes
freshly grated Parmesan cheese
Thai sweet basil, parsley, oregano or European basil

Serves 4–6

Heat the oil in a large frying pan or saucepan over low–medium heat and fry the celery, leek, onion and carrots for about 12 minutes. Add the beef and stir well until it's evenly browned.

Add the garlic, fortified wine and fish sauce and cook for 10 minutes. Add the fresh tomatoes, cover with a lid and cook for 15 minutes over medium heat.

Add the canned tomatoes, bay leaves, mushrooms and stock cube. Stir and simmer for 30–45 minutes.

Cook the spaghetti according to the package instructions. Drain and serve the bolognese sauce with the spaghetti.

Garnishes
Garnish with the Parmesan cheese, celery leaves and herbs.

Mango smoothie
sữa chua xoài

In April and May, mangoes are in season in Vietnam. The ones we get in England are a different variety, not as silky and sweet as the green Vietnamese ones, which are best when the skin has many black spots.

Mangoes are tropical fruits that grow in plenty of sunshine, therefore South East Asians believe they are very warming to the body. For this reason, eating too many mangoes can leave you with a sore throat and mean a restless night's sleep. As my mother would advise, only eat mangoes in moderation.

2 small, ripe mangoes
250 g/1 cup natural/plain
  yogurt
4 tablespoons sweetened
  condensed milk

Serves 2–4

Peel, stone/pit and chop the mangoes. Put in a blender or food processor with the yogurt, condensed milk and 500 ml/2 cups water. Blend until smooth. Serve immediately.

VARIATION Mango lassi ice cream
Peel, stone/pit and chop 2 ripe mangoes. Put in a blender or food processor with 500 g/2 cups natural/plain yogurt and 200 g/7 oz. sweetened condensed milk. Blend until smooth. Churn in an ice cream maker for 50 minutes. Freeze for at least 4 hours.

My mother has a real love for food and embraces all of its goodness. Because of her attention to this, her whole character is made of the perfect balance of yin and yang. True to Vietnamese form, her brothers and sisters insist on sending all her favourite foods over whenever they get the chance, as she lives to love and eat food. When my mother moved to London, she waited eagerly for letters from home. They usually arrived with a packet of basil seeds so that she could make our favourite drink, enjoyed in Vietnam for its refreshing, cooling effect and nutritional value. When immersed in water, the seeds develop a jelly-like coating. Bite down on them and the bubbles crunch and pop. The drink is usually flavoured with cane sugar or honey.

Basil seed drink
nước hạt é

3 tablespoons basil seeds
3 tablespoons honey

Makes 1 litre/4 cups

Mix the basil seeds, honey and 1 litre/4 cups water in a clear jug/pitcher and watch as the basil seeds form a translucent coating.

   Serve at room temperature or chilled.

Fried foods are a vice and we all love fried food sometimes. Banana fritters are my particular weakness. The hot, melty bananas fried in sweet coconut-rice-flour batter are the ultimate treat to devour in front of the television! The smell of a fritter street stall also drives me bananas! Bananas are the most important traditional fruit of Vietnam. They are grown and sold everywhere and used in many dessert dishes. One lady vendor had a cast-iron sandwich press to cook the banana fritters and presented me with one that resembled a toastie or crêpe. Vietnamese bananas are short, stubby, black and bruised (but not rotten or over-ripe) and incredibly sweet. For this recipe, just-ripe bananas work best.

Banana fritters
chuối chiến

6 just-ripe bananas
200 g/1½ cups rice flour
400 ml/1¾ cups coconut
  milk
100 g/½ cup (caster) sugar
dash of vanilla extract or
  seeds from 1 vanilla
  bean
4 tablespoons sunflower
  oil
icing/confectioners'
  sugar, to dust

Coconut custard
400 ml/1¾ cups coconut
  milk
1 teaspoon salt
1 teaspoon sugar

Serves 6–10

Cut the bananas in half lengthways, then chop them into 7-cm/3-inch pieces.

Mix together the rice flour, coconut milk, sugar and vanilla in a bowl, making sure it is smooth and free of lumps. Add the bananas and mix to coat in the batter.

Heat the oil in a frying pan over medium heat and fry the bananas, in batches, for 2–3 minutes on each side or until golden brown. Set aside on kitchen paper/paper towels.

Coconut custard
Put the coconut milk, salt and sugar in a saucepan over low heat and heat until warm.

Dust the fritters with icing/confectioners' sugar and serve warm or at room temperature with the coconut custard.

Celebrations and feasts

Vietnamese people love eating so much that they have a term, "*ăn chơi*" to mean "to eat playfully" or "snack". There are many small and light streetfood portions that you can pick up and eat on the go, throughout the day, every day.

During *tết*, the lunar new year, which celebrates the start of spring, snacks, candy, fruits, food gifts, cherry blossom and kumquat fill the house. This symbolizes fertility and fruitfulness for the family for the year and represents luck, good health and prosperity. They are also meant as offerings to ancestors and loved ones who have passed away, so that they live a healthy, prosperous and well-fed afterlife. Eating a feast (*ăn tết*) at this time is a major activity, with a range of modest peasant dishes like braised pork belly in coconut with eggs, and sticky rice cake with yellow bean and pork (*bánh chưng*). The family gathers and children

are given red envelopes with money, for luck. Traditional rituals are performed before *tết*, for example visiting the family altar or grave to give thanks; spring-cleaning the house to get rid of the old and usher in the new; paying off debts for a clean slate; and decorating the home for longevity.

Other big celebrations include weddings. Typically, they consist of a string of ceremonies beforehand, starting with an engagement party and continuing with offerings of symbolic fruits and foods to each of the families.

The glorious wedding day itself has three feasts, first at the bride's home, then at a restaurant for close family members, then an evening feast with friends, family and neighbours where an average of eight courses will be served.

During birthdays, the birthday person invites a suitable number of guests to dinner and often pays the bill.

In Phan Thiết, there lives a poet and teacher. Every day after school, he opens up his garden at the front of his old house, turns on the fairy lights hanging from a jackfruit tree and people flood inside for tea, coffee and *crème caramel* – the best in the world! I always visit this place when I go to Vietnam. It's a must! The poet does not say much about what goes into his famous dessert. He only tells a story of the love for his wife, his muse, whom he lost. She loved his *kem flan*, and he tells us that he makes it every day so that she can also enjoy it in her afterlife.

The Vietnamese love *crème caramel*, one of the things brought over by the French. In Vietnam, they do not really have ovens, so it is usually steamed.

Crème caramel
kem flan

Crème
120 ml/½ cup double/
   heavy cream
200 g/7 oz. sweetened
   condensed milk
250 ml/1 cup half-fat milk
1½ teaspoons vanilla
   extract
2 egg yolks
4 whole eggs

40 g/¼ cup (caster) sugar

Caramel
140 g/¾ cup (caster) sugar
100 ml/⅓ cup strong
   coffee

*20-cm/8-inch cake pan
   or 10 ramekins*

Serves 8–10

Crème
Preheat the oven to 160°C (325°F) Gas 3.
   Beat all the ingredients together in a bowl.

Caramel
Put the sugar and coffee in a saucepan over medium–high heat and stir to dissolve the sugar. Cook for 15–30 minutes. To test if the caramel is ready, drip a little in a ramekin with a spoon. If it hardens quickly, it is ready. If not, continue to cook and re-test.

   Once the caramel is ready, pour a thin layer into the cake pan or ramekins (enough to cover the base) and swirl around very quickly to coat the base before it sets. Allow to set and harden.

   If you are using a cake pan, pour the crème into it. If you are using ramekins, pour about 3 cm/1 inch of the crème into each ramekin. Place the pan/ramekins in a roasting pan and pour enough water in to come halfway up the pan/ramekins. This is a bain-marie and allows gentle and even baking. Bake in the oven for 20–25 minutes (ramekins) or 40 minutes (cake). Allow to cool, then chill for at 6 hours or overnight.

   To serve, run a thin knife all around the edge of the pan/ramekins. Turn it upside down onto a dish or bowl and tap it to help the dessert pop out. The caramel should drizzle down the sides, forming a puddle.

kem bơ

In South East Asia, avocado is usually consumed sweet. As it has a high (mostly monounsaturated) fat content, it is an important staple where fatty foods like dairy, fatty meat and fish are limited. At home, my preferred simple dessert is a ripe avocado smashed with a fork and mixed with a generous sprinkling of sugar – or better, sweetened condensed milk or honey.

In Vietnam, many street vendors sell fruit juices and smoothies day and night (especially at night). One of the most popular smoothies is avocado with sugar or condensed milk, or with other fruit juices that pair well like coconut or papaya. My mother always reminds me that avocados are very good for you. She regularly has a supply of avocados and makes sure we eat them as she believes they have all sorts of health benefits such as lowering cholesterol and being high in vitamins.

Avocado ice cream

2 ripe avocados
520 ml/2¼ cups coconut water
5 tablespoons sweetened condensed milk

ice cream maker (optional)

Serves 4–6

Peel, stone and chop the avocados. Put in a blender or food processor with the coconut water and condensed milk. Blend until smooth. If you do not have a blender or food processor, mash in a bowl with a potato masher or fork until smooth.

Churn in an ice cream maker for 1 hour. Freeze for at least 2 hours. If you do not have an ice cream maker, after freezing it for 2 hours, blend it again. Repeat at least twice over 2 days.

To serve as a smoothie, simply put the ingredients in a blender (with or without ice) and use only 4 tablespoons sweetened condensed milk. If you do not wish to use dairy, sweeten with sugar instead.

Vietnamese yogurt is consumed at any time of the day as a snack or dessert, even after a bowl of *phở* for breakfast. It can be frozen, a drink over crushed ice, or as it comes in a jar. This is the taste of my childhood. Its simple zesty taste combined with creamy condensed milk is a perfect palate cleanser.

Frozen yogurt kem da-ua

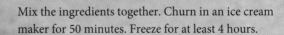

500 g/2 cups natural/plain yogurt
300 g/10½ oz. sweetened condensed milk

ice cream maker

Makes 1 litre/4 cups

Mix the ingredients together. Churn in an ice cream maker for 50 minutes. Freeze for at least 4 hours.

Yogurt da-ua

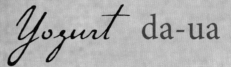

NOTE Vietnamese people do not really use measuring devices: it is all done by ratios of cans, containers and spoons

1 can (400 g/14 oz.) sweetened condensed milk

1 can boiling water
2 cans room-temperature water
½ can sweetened UHT milk
2 cans natural/plain yogurt

several clean, small jars or yogurt pots

Makes about 2 litres/8 cups

Mix all the ingredients together in a large bowl, using the empty can of condensed milk to measure the ingredients. Divide between the jars or yogurt pots and cover with clingfilm/plastic wrap.

Put the yogurt pots in a container that will fit inside another larger container. Pour enough boiling water into the larger container to come halfway up the smaller one. Cover with a lid and carefully wrap in a plastic bag. Leave for at least 3 hours in a warm spot (or more if it's cold) for the yogurt to ferment. Serve chilled.

Pandan leaves are used to colour food. When cooked, they have a distinctively refreshing flavour – rosy, almondy and grassy – and are used frequently for desserts, much as vanilla extract is. They are also delicious infused in hot water as a beverage. This cake recipe is light and fluffy and lovely. Cakes like these are usually enjoyed for dessert at birthday gatherings and other celebrations.

Pandan cake
bánh bông lan lá dứa

8 eggs
130 g/⅔ cup (caster) sugar
1 teaspoon cream of tartar
80 g/3 oz. pandan leaves, chopped
80 ml/⅓ cup sunflower oil
1 teaspoon baking powder
1 teaspoon green food colouring or pandan essence (optional)
100 g/¾ cup plain/ all-purpose flour

Decoration
400 g/2¾ cups icing/ confectioners' sugar
4 teaspoons pandan essence
grated zest of 3 limes

non-stick 22–24-cm/9-inch ring cake pan, greased evenly with oil (if you use any other pan, the cake will sink)

Serves 8–10

Preheat the oven to 200°C (400°F) Gas 6.

Separate the eggs and put the yolks in one mixing bowl and the whites in another. Add the sugar and cream of tartar to the egg whites and whisk with an electric whisk in one continuous direction only (such as clockwise) until the whites are stiff.

Put the pandan leaves and 150 ml/⅔ cup water in a blender and process until quite smooth. Sieve/strain the mixture into the bowl of egg yolks and add the oil, baking powder and green colouring or pandan essence. Whisk for about 5 minutes or until paler and doubled in volume. Sift the flour into the bowl and fold in with a large spoon.

Add half the stiffened egg whites to the bowl and fold in gently. Now add the remaining egg whites and gently fold in one direction.

When ready to bake, heat the prepared cake pan in the oven for 1 minute or until slightly warm to the touch. Pour the mixture into the warm pan and bake in the preheated oven for 30–45 minutes.

Turn the cake upside onto a wire rack, leave the pan in place and allow to cool completely. Once cool, carefully remove the pan.

Decoration
Put the sugar, pandan essence and 100 ml/⅓ cup water in a bowl and mix together until smooth. Drizzle over the cake and sprinkle with lime zest.

Index

Thank you

Thank you to Má Nga, my beautiful, wonderful mother, for showing me and my brother her love through food; for always gifting our mouths and hearts with all the delightful tastes of home; for truly providing us with a grounding sense of belonging; for always watching over my shoulder to make sure I have the right balance of flavours; and for always being there to support all my crazy dreams and ideas.

Thank you to Céline Hughes, Megan Smith and all at RPS for taking a chance on this maverick and publishing my first book, which has made my childhood dreams come true. My agent, Chris Wellbelove at Greene & Heaton, for believing in me, working hard with me and putting up with my diva outbreaks. Gail Doggett for all the tips and advice on writing the initial book proposal. Will Timbers for his English(ness) and helping me with mine. Thank you to Will Hodson for hearing and loving all the stories.

Thank you to Clare Winfield with whom I had the time of my life photographing this book, whom I learned so much from, who has given this book so much of her love and made it even more beautiful than I could have ever imagined. Thanks to Jo Harris for some amazing props. Thank you to Rosie Birkett for assisting on set and making us smile and laugh throughout and for being an incredible dear friend.

Thank you to the kind and marvellous Chef Raymond Blanc for his foreword. It means the world to me to have support from a great master. And thank you to Ching-He Huang for all the encouragements.

Thank you to everyone who has supported me and been to my supper club and cooking classes, and to the lovely Leluu girls who are always the root and strength of everything I do.

Thank you to G Blair for helping me see with my eyes closed as well as wide open. Thank you to my wonderful, loyal and loving friends who cooked, tested and ate the recipes and gave much valuable feedback from London to Sydney. It is my friends who are my family and who inspire me to cook, to share and to enjoy every bit of this delicious life.